A WOMAN'S VERSION OF
THE FAUST LEGEND

A WOMAN'S VERSION OF
THE FAUST LEGEND

The Seven Strings of the Lyre by George Sand

Translated into English,

with Introduction and Notes

by George A. Kennedy

*The
University of
North Carolina
Press*

*Chapel Hill
and London*

The paper in this book meets the guidelines for per-
manence and durability of the Committee on Production Guidelines for Book Longevity of the Council on
Library Resources.

Printed in the United States of America

93 92 91 90 89 5 4 3 2 1

Library of Congress Cataloging-in-Publication Data

Sand, George, 1804–1876.
  A Woman's Version of the Faust Legend: *The Seven
  Strings of the Lyre* by George Sand

  Translation of: Les sept cordes de la lyre.
  Bibliography: p.
  Includes index.
  I. Title. II. Title: Seven strings of the lyre.
PO2411.S313 1989   842'.7   88-33796
ISBN 0-8078-1856-9 (alk. paper)

I am very grateful to Iris Tillman Hill, Editor-in-Chief
of the University of North Carolina Press, for the interest she has taken in this work, to the copyeditor,
Pamela Upton, and to the designer, April Leidig-
Higgins, as well as to other members of the staff of
the University of North Carolina Press who have
contributed to its publication and distribution.
G.A.K.

TO BERTHE M. MARTI
who for twenty-five years has challenged, inspired,
and befriended her colleagues and students
at the University of North Carolina

 *Contents*

 A WOMAN'S VERSION OF
THE FAUST LEGEND

 *Introduction*

This curious work came to my attention when I was studying appearances of Helen of Troy, or of fictional characters named Helen, in European literature. Though the play is, of course, known to students of nineteenth-century French and to experts on George Sand, its audience has been little wider. Yet it is potentially of some interest to a variety of readers. No English translation has ever been published, and I offer one in hopes of making the work more accessible to American students.

The Seven Strings of the Lyre is a reaction by a major French writer to Goethe's *Faust* and one of the very few treatments of the Faust legend by a woman (another is Dorothy Sayers's 1939 play, *The Devil to Pay*). It was written in 1838 during the early stages of Sand's romantic liaison with Frédéric Chopin, and one of its themes is the nature of music: the ability of music to express ideas, and its relationship to other arts. One character in the work may be thought to represent Chopin and another, to a more limited extent, Franz Liszt. Sand's treatment of music seems to have been inspired by recent discussions with Liszt. The work thus has a small place in the history of romantic aesthetics and musicology. Philosophically, and this is a very philosophic work, it is a reaction against eighteenth-century rationalism—the tradition of Cartesianism and Voltaire—and an assertion of the existence of some higher truth to be found in music, poetry, and a sympathetic response to nature. As often in Sand's novels, this higher vision is most easily obtained by a woman innocent of the complexities and pedantry of learning, but the lot of women is suffering, and the threat of a brutalizing marriage hangs over them, as Sand knew from personal experience. Yet a woman may lead a man to fuller knowledge and a fuller life through love.

Politically, *The Lyre* presents an idealized socialism in the tradition of Rousseau and the Saint-Simoneans, founded on faith in the perfectibility of human society and hostile to both the aristocracy of the *ancien régime* and the bourgeois monarchy of Louis-Philippe. Though deeply romantic, it is also opposed to the art-for-art's-sake romanticism of Gautier and other writers of the time in that it demands social responsibility of an artist. In Sand's view, the arts should lead society to awareness of truth, freedom, and the meaning of life, and this is what she here attempts to do. The primary value of the work is as a document in literary, aesthetic, and intellectual history. As a purely literary achievement it falls below many of Sand's novels and plays, but her technical skills of composition were always great. With minor exceptions identified in the notes, the plot is well worked out, the characters are vividly realized, some of the scenes are dramatically effective, and at times Helen and the Spirit of the Lyre rise to a poetic eloquence that may move those readers who can enter into the romantic mind of the early nineteenth century. Sand has attempted a difficult task: to cast into words the effect of music and to give dramatic interest to philosophical abstractions. Readers of the work, both at the time of publication and since, have usually thought that she was only partially successful, but the attempt deserves respect, and *The Lyre* makes an interesting contrast to Sand's treatment of similar themes elsewhere.

GEORGE SAND

George Sand (1804–1876) was one of the most prolific writers of all time; her published works, chiefly fiction and drama, ran to over one hundred volumes before her death, not counting articles in journals. Other pieces have been published since, of which the most important is the voluminous correspondence she conducted with friends, lovers, publishers, and relatives throughout her life, supplying a fascinating, detailed picture of the circles in which she moved and of her own personality. She was born Aurore Dupin, daughter of an officer in Napoleon's army; her father died as a result of a fall from his horse when Aurore was four years old. She was largely raised by her strong-minded, aristocratic grandmother, Marie Dupin, though she spent periods with her own flighty, plebeian mother, Sophie, and three years as a student at the English convent in Paris. In 1823 she married Casimir Dudevant; they were ill-matched in almost every way and separated in 1831, after which she began to support herself by writing. Her early works were written in collaboration with Jules Sandeau and were published under the name Jules Sand. She adopted the name George Sand when she published her first important novel, *Indiana*, in 1832. The name George is apparently an allusion to Virgil's *Georgics* and a reflection of her love of country life (*georgos* in Greek means farmer). She never married again, but contracted a series of passionate relationships with men, of whom the best known are the poet Alfred de Musset and the composer-pianist Frédéric Chopin. Her more platonic friends included most major figures in the French artistic, musical, and literary worlds of the nineteenth century, among them Honoré de Balzac, Eugène Delacroix, Alexandre Dumas, Gustave Flaubert, Théophile Gautier, Franz Liszt, and Charles-Augustin Sainte-Beuve. Most of her time was spent in Paris or at her country home at Nohant in Berry, but she traveled at

various times in Spain, Italy, and Switzerland, and she seems
to have had a good knowledge of Italian and English. She did
not know German, at least not well enough to read German
literature in the original, though she had a number of German
friends, including Heinrich Heine. As a consequence, her
knowledge of Goethe's works, including *Faust*, was derived
from French translations and secondary sources. (For addi-
tional biographical information, the reader should refer to
works listed in the Select Bibliography at the end of this
volume.)

In the twentieth century, interest in George Sand's life has
often overshadowed interest in her writings. In moving out
of a conventional marriage into open, public, erotic relationships with men, who were often younger than herself, she
deeply shocked the bourgeois society of her time and has become something of a model to women of later generations in
their search for independence. In her books, letters, and conversation she opened up her feelings, hopes, and fears in a
way that, to my knowledge, no woman had done before. Although she created a career for herself as a writer, it was not
the desire for a career that originally motivated her search
for independence; rather, the coarseness and emptiness of her
marriage seem to have moved her to seek a fuller experience
of life. Writing became her source of income, and in the process the expression of her experience through writing became
of vital importance to her. She differs from her friends Balzac
and Flaubert, and among later French writers she might be
said somewhat to resemble Proust in that she rarely affects
objectivity. Among the causes she took up, the most fruitful
was the sympathetic portrayal of the life of the French peas-
ant, a life that to her was often beautiful and endowed with a
profound, if unverbalized, understanding of the meaning of
life. She describes this program in the prefatory material to *La
mare au diable* (1842) and carried it through in a series of pas-

toral novels that are perhaps her finest writing, characterized by wholesomeness, sincerity, and grace. But she could write on the grand scale as well, as in *The Countess of Rudolstadt*, where she unfolds the most improbable succession of events in such a way that they seem not only credible but logically necessary. Many of her books begin as romantic love stories for popular consumption, but at some point, whether in the portrayal of character and motivation, in the handling of incident, or in reflection on the action, some insight emerges that raises an otherwise shallow tale to the level of *belles lettres*.

SAND'S *LYRE* AND GOETHE'S *FAUST*

The Seven Strings of the Lyre (*Les septs cordes de la lyre*) is a philosophical play, not intended for production on stage, written in simple but poetic prose in the late summer of 1838, soon after the beginning of Sand's relationship with Chopin. It was published in *La Revue des deux mondes*, a journal to which Sand was then under contract, in the issues of 15 April and 1 May 1839, then as a separate book by F. Bonnaire in Paris in 1840 and in later collected editions of Sand's works. The translation below is based primarily on the 1869 edition in the *Oeuvres complètes de George Sand*, but I have also consulted a copy of the original edition in the University of North Carolina Library, autographed by George Sand "à mon ami Henry Harrisse, Paris, 8 juin '75," and the modern French edition of René Bourgeois, which has a valuable introduction.

The time and place of the action of *The Lyre* are not specified in the stage directions. The time, however, is clearly the present or recent past, thus about 1838: the reigning king in act 1, scene 7, much resembles Louis-Philippe; Helen's vision of the earth in act 4, scene 1, includes steam locomotives and railways, a development of the 1830s; in act 3, scene 3, the eighteenth century is referred to as the past. The place is less consistently maintained. Throughout most of the action it appears to be a small German university town where Albertus is a teacher of philosophy: the students and townspeople have German names; the countryside is nearby; people seem to know others in a way not characteristic of large cities. This is clearly adopted from the Faust legend. But the scenes mentioned above as fixing the time of the action are inconsistent with such a location, for act 1, scene 7, seems to suggest that the city is a royal residence, and the first of Helen's views from the cathedral tower in act 4, scene 1, seems clearly to overlook Paris. Yet the cathedral cannot be Notre-Dame de Paris, for its high bell tower is surmounted by a tapering spire. Strasbourg Cathedral would better fit the description. Clearly, although the basic setting is a German-speaking university town, Sand freely departs from this locale to bring in contemporary French allusions.

The action of the play describes the efforts of the devil, Mephistopheles (Méphistophélès), to win the soul of Master Albertus (Maître Albertus); the latter, as Mephistopheles tells us in act 1, scene 3, is a descendant of Faust and perhaps also of Faust's mistress, Marguerite. To reach his goal, Mephistopheles discovers he must first destroy a remarkable lyre in Albertus's possession, "the symbol that here lights the flames of the heart," and secure the spirit that dwells within the lyre. His task is aided by the fact that the middle-aged Albertus has come to feel that, in his dedication to philosophy, life and love have passed him by; it is complicated, however, by differences between Albertus's character and that of Faust ("He has more conscience than the other; pride has taken greater hold of him, vanity none"), by the fact that the lyre is magical and cannot be broken by the agents the devil first tries to employ, and by the presence of Helen (Hélène).

Helen of Troy is a traditional character in the Faust legend (derived from stories of Helen and Faustus in early Christian accounts of Simon Magus), and is often a *femme fatale* conjured up from hell to awaken Faust's passions and secure his damnation. This is the role she plays in Christopher Marlowe's *Doctor Faustus*, in which she appears but never speaks. In the second part of Goethe's *Faust*, however, she plays a benign role as a symbol of the beauty and naturalness of classical antiquity, and her union with Faust represents the synthesis of the classic and antique with the Gothic and Germanic. In Sand's play, Helen is a beautiful young woman who has come to live with Albertus as his ward on the death of her father, Meinbaker the instrument maker. Her only inheritance is the magic lyre, made by her ancestor Adelsfreit. Albertus has sought to teach her philosophy, but she is bewildered by books. Her intelligence responds instead to nature, to virtue, and to music, and in the course of the play she achieves and expresses a knowledge of God and understanding of nature, a sympathy for human life and suffering, and finally love, which is impossible within the system of rational philosophy. She awakens the love of the Spirit of the Lyre and ultimately frees him from his prison and thus from the clutches of Mephistopheles. She also innocently awakens the love of Albertus. Mephistopheles has sought to encourage this as a way of leading Albertus into fleshly lust or disgusting him by a degradation of Helen, but he is ultimately unsuccessful. Albertus learns from Helen what he had never learned from books, and though she departs with the Spirit of the Lyre to the heavenly empyrean and the infinite, Albertus is left with a new motivation to study and to teach a more profound and more sensitive view of philosophy.

George Sand's judgment of Goethe, influenced by her mentor at the time, Pierre Leroux, is set out in an article entitled "Essai sur le drame fantastique," which she published in *La Revue des deux mondes* at the end of 1839, a year after her composition of *The Lyre* (see the article by Bourgeois, listed in the Select Bibliography). Sand viewed Goethe as an able artist and *Faust* as a considerable achievement, but she felt Goethe was lacking in "enthusiasm, belief, and passion." To her, he was not an ideal poet, for she thought he himself lacked an ideal, and she regarded him as a skeptic and as a German descendant of Voltaire. She also identified him with the art-for-art's-sake movement as she knew it in France and criticized him for a lack of social conscience. Some of her views clearly influenced her recasting of the Faust story in *The Lyre*. She criticizes Goethe's Mephistopheles as not adequately wicked; her character showed what a devil should be. She finds Goethe's Faust, as a character, too cold; her Albertus is considerably more emotional. For Goethe's simple village girl, Marguerite, or for the dangerous Helen of the earlier Faust legend, she substituted the angelic Helen, who becomes the central figure in the action.

Sand seems to have based her judgments on a reading of the first part of *Faust* and of the separately published Helen Act in part two during the spring of 1838. The complete second part of *Faust*, first published in German in 1832, did not appear in French until the version by Henri Blaze in 1840. If Sand had known the complete part two of *Faust*, her judgments, especially of Goethe's social conscience, might well have been different, for it is in the later part of the work that Faust commits himself to service to society. On the positive side, Goethe's portrayal of Euphorion may possibly have influenced Sand's conception of the Spirit of the Lyre. Although the two are rather different in character, Euphorion, the offspring of Faust and Helen, is the personification of poetry and is associated with music, and he is reminiscent of Lord Byron much as the Spirit can be regarded as reminiscent of Chopin. (For Sand's frequent use of Goethe in her other works, see Baldensperger's survey, *Goethe en France*, listed in the Select Bibliography.)

MUSIC AND PHILOSOPHY

Music was an important part of George Sand's life. In her autobiography, *My Life*, she tells of a small harp that she had in her student days, and she also played the piano. Her serious interest in music was enhanced by conversations and correspondence with Franz Liszt in 1836 (see Marix-Spire, pp. 470, 484–85). Liszt may appear in *The Lyre* as the student Hanz, who has a special understanding of music. When Helen plays the lyre, the other characters hear only the music of the instrument, but Sand verbalizes the meaning for the benefit of the reader, implying that musical sounds convey ideas, both abstract and concrete. Moreover, music and words are analogous to visual images; being is both a harmony and a prism. Liszt, however, did not like the play. He wrote later that it left "a painful impression" and spoke of its "lassitude, enervation, and decadence" (Marix-Spire, pp. 561–62). What Chopin thought, I do not know. Immediately after Sand completed *The Lyre* he went with her for the winter to Majorca, already showing signs of tuberculosis and under pressure to complete some compositions for his publishers. The unconventional couple was not well received on the island, the climate was less agreeable than they expected, and they both had a difficult winter.

Music and musicians appear in a number of Sand's works, for example *Consuelo* (1842–43), which centers around the life of an opera singer. In *Les maîtres sonneurs* (1857) Sand tells the story of a young man who seems taciturn and dull but who is able, by playing the bagpipes, to convey thoughts, resemblances, and moods. Her heroines, like Helen, are often intelligent, sensitive people with a feeling for nature and the arts who, despite lack of formal education, have wisdom, insight, and understanding. A good example is found in one of her last novels, *Marianne*.

The songs of Helen and the Spirit of the Lyre adumbrate a system of philosophy, though many of the details remain vague. The seven strings of the lyre together speak the harmony of all being. The two golden strings sing of the mystery of the infinite, one being identified with the ideal and with intelligence, the other with faith and the ardor of the soul, as explained in act 2, scene 4. When Albertus, urged on by Mephistopheles, has disconnected these strings, Helen plays the silver strings, which sing of terrestrial creation and nature. The first silver string is dedicated to the contemplation of nature, the second to Providence (see act 3, scene 3.) After Albertus disconnects the silver strings, Helen plays the steel strings, and the Spirit now sings of the grandeur and genius of man, while Helen sings of man's crimes and misfortunes (see act 4, scene 3.) With the removal of the steel strings there remains one brazen string (*corde d'airain*) that sings of love.

Antecedents for the metaphysics here expressed can be found in Platonism, in writings of Spinoza, and in the mysticism of the seventeenth and eighteenth centuries, especially in the writings of Emanuel Swedenborg, but more immediate sources for George Sand are the writings and conversations she had with Hughes Felicité de Lamennais (1782–1854) and especially with Pierre Leroux (1797–1848) (see Evans, esp. pp. 38–43.) Leroux's treatise *De l'humanité*, though not published until 1840, represents his teaching at this time. It sets out a view of life as aspiration and speaks of an indivisible trinity of sensation, sentiment, and reason, moving through history toward an eventual perfection. Death is a veil that separates us from a new phenomenal manifestation and a new knowledge of man, and we eventually return to God, who contains our latent being. In a letter to Ferdinand Guillon in 1844 (*Correspondance*, 4, no. 2835), Sand describes herself as "only a pale reflection of Leroux, a fantastic disciple of the same ideal, but a disciple mute and ravished before his word, always ready to throw in the fire all her works, to write, to think, to pray, and to act under his inspiration." She claims, with considerable exaggeration, that she only seeks to translate into novels the philosophy of her master. I say "exaggeration" because it seems to me that Sand's most important inspiration lay in her own experience and its imaginative development. What Leroux provided her was a conceptualization of what she already instinctively believed.

The lyre, as a symbol of the union of music and poetry, was already a commonplace in classical times, for example in the poetry of Pindar or Horace, and the figure of the broken or unstrung lyre is occasionally found as well. One example that George Sand would have known occurs in book 2, chapter 3, of Victor Hugo's *Notre-Dame de Paris* (1831), in which a woman's voice interrupts the song of the Bohemian and Grégoire exclaims, "Cursed notched saw that comes to break the lyre!" The specific source, however, for a lyre on which different strings have different meanings apparently came to Sand from Michel de Bourges, whom she called "Everard." Among his papers was found a sketch of a lyre with the inscription "The lyre of George Sand after the plan of her friend Everard. Nohant, 11 August 1835." This date is exactly three years before composition of *The Lyre*. On the strings are the following labels: (1) peace, sciences, agriculture; (2) war or liberty and tyranny; (3) sufferings or death, crime; (4) joys, or belief, the martyrs, virtue; (5) evocation, tombs; (6) love of the elements; the sea, the sky, the earth, water, fire; (7) God, or prayer, and adoration (see Karénine, 2:379–80). Sand has apparently rearranged the ideas into a different sequence, but most of the motifs appear at some point in the songs of Helen and the Spirit.

The lyre as described in the play is perhaps technically a cithara, a larger and more resonant instrument than the classical lyre. Its base is a sound box that the player grasps in her left arm or rests on her knee. Perpendicular to the sound box rise two curved arms, joined at the top by a bar with pegs, making an instrument about two feet square. The seven strings are drawn up from the sound box over a bridge to the pegs. The frame is elaborately decorated with inlaid ivory figures, as described in act 1, scene 7. Such lyres were best known to Sand and her friends from representation in classical and neoclassical art, but the eighteenth century had seen an interest in new forms, and Adelsfreit's creation should perhaps be thought of as part of that development. In a treatise entitled *Lyra Barberina*, published in 1763, Giovanni Battista Doni gave an account, with illustrations, of the lyre's history and of his invention of a new nineteen-stringed version. Other innovations included what are known as the viol-lyre and the lyre-guitar.

THE CHARACTERS

It seems possible that the Spirit of the Lyre, imprisoned in the instrument, in some sense represents Frédéric Chopin. Whatever Sand's conscious intent, such an identification is reasonable on the part of a reader. The Spirit of the Lyre, like Chopin, speaks with music; Helen, with whom Sand herself may be identified, alone fully understands him. A harmony and unity emerge in their thought, they learn from each other and come to love one another, and together they escape from the constraints and suffering of the world into an ideal union of bliss and harmony. In contrast to them are the worldly poet,

painter, composer, and critic of act 1, scene 7; these are carica-
tures of professional types and apparently do not satirize specific individuals.

The figure of Albertus evokes many connotations. He is
called a descendant of Faust and is, first of all, Sand's version
of that traditional character. He may in part be modeled on
philosophers Sand knew, for example Lamennais, and he may
even incorporate some memories of her tutor, François Des-
chartres, who had tried to teach her Latin and who dabbled
in theology, medicine, and magic. The choice of Albertus in
its Latin form, however, easily recalls Albertus Magnus (ca.
1206–1280), scholastic philosopher and theologian, an arche-
type of the man of learning of the past. He is cast in the latter
role in Edgar Quinet's epic, *Ahasvérus* (1833). Another Albert
in Sand's mind at this time was Count Albert Grzymala (1793–
1855), a Polish émigré, a close friend of Chopin, and a confi-
dant to Sand in her relationship with the composer, as her
letters indicate. Albertus has nothing of Grzymala's character,
but that he had made some contribution to the work is suggested by the strange quotation Sand set on the first page of
The Lyre. It purports to be Grzymala's translation of a Slavic
(Polish?) song in which there is reference to the Son of the
Lyre, Spirits of Light, and Spirits of Harmony. Thus some of
the figures of the play are attributed to Grzymala. The quotation is very unlike any Slavic folk poetry, and no such translation by Grzymala is otherwise known. Perhaps there is some
private allusion here; something Grzymala had said may have
met a response in Sand's thinking. The song is addressed to
an unidentified "Eugene," but it is interesting that "Eugene"
and "Albert," the one Greek in origin, the other Germanic,
have the same basic meaning of "well-born."

There are still other Alberts who have some connection with
The Lyre or with how it might be read in Sand's circle. If *The
Lyre* is in part a reaction to Goethe's *Faust*, it is also in some

sense a response to writings by Théophile Gautier, and especially to his role as a leading spokesman in the art-for-art's-
sake movement. Although George Sand and Gautier (1811–
1872) were not especially intimate, they knew each other and
had many friends in common. In 1832 Gautier had published
Albertus, or the Soul and Sin, a narrative poem in 122 stanzas.
As a result, some of his friends gave him the nickname "Albertus." In Gautier's poem, a wicked woman named Véronique, by nature ugly in the extreme, disguises herself to appear young and beautiful, magically transforms her black cat
into the figure of Don Juan, and goes to live in Leyden, where
she becomes the mysterious center of a luxurious, hedonistic
circle. Albertus is a young painter obsessed with memories
of a beautiful woman he had known in Venice (where Sand
had lived with Musset a few years earlier). He is summoned
to Véronique's home, instantly falls in love with her, and declares that to possess her he would give his soul to the devil
(stanza 94). In a highly erotic scene, she offers herself to him,
but at the moment of sexual climax, naked in his arms, she
suddenly turns back into the hideous old woman she really
is. One might compare this scene with Mephistopheles' experience with the beautiful Lamiae in Goethe's *Faust* (pt. 2,
l. 7770). Albertus then discovers himself in a filthy room with
Don Juan, who has again become a cat, "like the dog of Faust,"
and who ties him in magic bonds with his black tail, from
which radiates a strange blue light. There follows an assembly
in hell before the devil, accompanied by a fiendish symphony
of cacophonous music. The end of act 2, scene 7, of *The Lyre*
could recall this scene. Albertus's soul is lost, and in the morning his dead body is found on the Appian Way near Rome.
In the last stanza the narrator speaks of the poem as an "allegory" but coyly leaves its interpretation to the reader. The
sensuality and irony of the poem really make it a parody of a
moral allegory. In the last line the narrator calls for a volume

of Rabelais' *Pantagruel*, thereby seeming to assert the spirit of Rabelaisian humor and its intoxication with life.

Again, in a story entitled "Celle-ci et celle-là," included in *Les jeunes France* (1833), Gautier introduced a central character named Albert, a sophisticated young man who, on the last page, is ironically described as "true reason, intimate friend of true poetry, himself fine and delicate prose who holds at his finger tips poetry that wishes to fly from the solid earth of reality into clouds of dreams and chimeras. He is Don Juan who gives a hand to Childe-Harold." Sand may have amused herself by taking the name of a character twice identified with Gautier and inverting the presentation for her own purposes. In 1836 Gautier published *Mademoiselle de Maupin*, the most brilliant and controversial novel of the period, immediately preceding Sand's composition of *The Lyre*. Its long preface is one of the most famous romantic declarations of art for art's sake, and the novel throughout is sensuous, physical, and amoral. Although there is no Albert in this story, there are some passages that provide background for Sand's *Lyre*. The narrator says, for example, "What use is a lyre without strings to a poet, or life without love to a man?" (chap. 2). And the description of moonlight, in chapter 4, bears some resemblance to the passage about the moon in act 3 of *The Lyre*.

Sand fundamentally disagreed with Gautier's view of art. Some of the issues of this disagreement are brought out in the debate between the poet, the painter, the composer, and the critic in act 1, scene 7 (perhaps the best single scene in *The Lyre*), and *The Lyre* as a whole is an example of the use of literature for philosophical and social purposes that Gautier rejected. The name "Albertus" thus draws attention to the difference. Sand again used the name "Albert" for the philosopher in *Consuelo* and its sequel, *The Countess of Rudolstadt*. Yet Gautier so wittily undercuts any serious meaning in his own treatments that the philosophizing on art and love in *The*

Lyre—especially to an audience that had enjoyed his poem, story, and novel—could easily have seemed strained, prudish, and now even irrelevant. The reaction was indeed generally negative. It is a mark of Sand's basic seriousness, and of her naiveté, that she expected *The Lyre* to be an artistic success in the aftermath of *Mademoiselle de Maupin*.

Gautier may be said, however, to have paid her the compliment of imitation much later in his short 1865 novel, *Spirite*, a very uncharacteristic and not very successful work that takes up some of *The Lyre*'s themes. In *Spirite*, a young nobleman, Guy de Malivert, falls in love with a spirit (actually a deceased young woman who had secretly loved him in life). Her love of him is sometimes expressed through music, and he calls her playing of the piano a comment on her words, analogous in color and sentiment, that prolong the passage in sonorous or melancholy vibrations. Spirite's playing is said to surpass the music of Chopin or Liszt, and just as Helen plays without touching the strings of the lyre, Spirite plays without touching the keys. Eventually Malivert and Spirite are, like Helen and the Spirit of the Lyre, joined in the spirit world. Swedenborgianism is an explicit theme in this story, and since some of the ideas of *The Lyre* resemble those of Swedenborg, that too can be thought of as a link between the two works.

PUBLICATION AND RECEPTION OF *THE LYRE*

On 8 August 1838, Sand wrote to Christine Buloz, wife of her publisher, François Buloz, reporting that though she was having difficulty completing the last twenty pages of *Spiridion* she had instead written about half of "a little fantastic drama," which was to become *The Lyre*. "I have been passionately working on it for five or six nights, and I can promise you that in a week at the most you will have it" (*Correspondance*, 4, no. 1775). Sand often did much of her writing at night and seems to have required little sleep. The half she had written, she pointed out, would be enough for one issue of *La Revue des deux mondes*, to which she was under contract.

It was not until 7 September, however, that she announced completion of *The Lyre* in a letter to Félix Bonnaire, again describing the work as "a kind of fantastic drama" (*Correspondance*, 4, no. 1784). She wanted Buloz to announce it and to publish it before *Spiridion*. Problems arose, however. Buloz did not like the play; it was too mystical and philosophical, and he was especially uncomfortable with the passage in act 1, scene 7, describing "the king's" preference for picture-frames over the pictures themselves. This could be easily taken as ridicule of Louis-Philippe's collection at Versailles, and was probably so intended. Buloz at the time was seeking appointment from the king as commissioner of the Comédie française. At the beginning of October, Sand wrote a curt note to Buloz demanding immediate publication before she left Paris on 20 October. She also asked for payment of "five to six thousand francs" (*Correspondance*, 4, no. 1790).

Although Buloz continued to postpone publication, by 15 February 1839 he had paid Sand five thousand francs for *The Lyre* (*Correspondance*, 4, no. 1827). On 17 March, Sand assured Charlotte Marliani that *The Lyre* was actually going to appear and was as suitable for the review as any other material, though "our Buloz hesitates and recoils because there are five or six passages too risky and because the dear man fears to embroil himself with our dear government" (*Correspondance*, 4, no. 1843), but later that month she again wrote to Buloz revealing the fear that he would renege and questioning his literary judgment (*Correspondance*, 4, no. 1846). At the beginning of April, now in Marseilles, she told Charlotte to assure

Buloz that she was writing a novel "to his taste," but first
he must pay her something on the account he owed her and
must publish *The Lyre* (*Correspondance*, 4, no. 1850).

By about 19 April, Sand had seen the first installment of *The
Lyre* and wrote to Emmanuel Arago asking him to proofread
the second half. The first half, she said, somewhat tongue-in-
cheek, "must have bored you to death, for you are too much
a beast to understand anything of this sublime, monumen-
tal, pyramidal, amazing, luxuriant, and lavish work. What follows, though ravishing, is less remarkable, and as a result will
displease you less." She was particularly nervous that Buloz
would tamper with the scene where Helen appears on the cathedral tower and sees all humanity spread out before her. He
would not believe that Helen could see so far, and Sand made
fun of his weak eyes. "You must understand," she said, "that I
attach some importance to these four or five lines [actually as
many pages]. I have continued to work for this ignoble journal
only on the condition that I have the most complete liberty"
(*Correspondance*, 4, no. 1857).

Pierre Leroux had corrected the proofs of act 1, but apparently act 2 had not been carefully corrected by anybody. Sand
complained to Buloz about it on 21 April, saying that she had
marked out how the pages ought to be set so that the reader
would understand that when Helen is in ecstasy the sound of
the lyre, but not her words, are heard by the other characters
(*Correspondance*, 4, no. 1859). Buloz was to ask Arago to proofread the remaining pages, if Leroux was still away. In a concil-
iatory tone, she told Buloz that he knew French better than
she did, but he didn't have time for this task. In any event,
nobody else was even to see the proofs except Buloz and his
wife—the latter in case they were useful in curing her insom-
nia! Writing to Buloz on 23 June, however, she was in a bitter
mood over his treatment of her. He pretended to understand
what he edited! She was very doubtful that he could under-

stand the second part of *Faust*, and she offered to pay him for all the money he had lost on *The Lyre*. "I'm not the jew Shylock, and I don't know what I would do with your skin," she says (*Correspondance*, 4, no. 1888). Buloz had written earlier that he did not like the second part of *Faust* any better than *The Lyre*. Writing again in December, she waived any payment for her new novel, *Pauline*: "I believe I owe it to you to make up for the bad success of *The Lyre*, which rests on my conscience" (*Correspondance*, 4, no. 1971).

Publication of *The Lyre* was greeted with silence by the critics, though Sand's productivity was so great it was easily overlooked in the flood of other works she was turning out, and its failure had no adverse effects on her reputation. Almost the only person who admired it was a young poet named Leconte de Lisle. In a short poem dedicated to George Sand (1839) he addressed her as "mystic Helen," and in the socialist journal *La Phalange* (2 [July 1845]: 179–82), he published his own "Hélène," inspired by *The Lyre*. In this work, he imagines a trip to Greece, where he is moved by the landscape and the art to a new vision of humanity. But subsequently Leconte de Lisle disowned the poem and, in authoritative editions of his works, replaced it with a new "Hélène," composed in 1852. In the new version, Helen of Troy has become the symbol of black destiny, the pessimism that the poet felt about politics and society when the Revolution of 1848 failed to advance his ideals. He turned to a view of art for art's sake and became a major figure in the Parnasse movement.

It should be noted that there are many "Helens" in nineteenth-century French literature, art, and music, though they appear to have been little influenced by Helen as she appears in *The Lyre*. The most famous is Offenbach's *La belle Hélène* (1864), which produced a series of reactions, including Jules Lemaître's charming comedy, *La bonne Hélène* (1897). Helen is also a character in Anatole France's *Thaïs*, and in Flaubert's

Temptation of Saint Anthony, as well as the subject of poems
by Théodore de Banville, Stéphane Mallarmé, and Paul Valéry. She was repeatedly painted by Gustave Moreau. The best-
known later version of the Faust theme in French literature
is probably Valéry's incomplete drama, *Mon Faust* (1946), in
which Helen is replaced by Faust's secretary, Lust. Two great
French operas are based on part 1 of Goethe's *Faust* (and thus
do not introduce Helen): *The Damnation of Faust* by Hector Berlioz (1854) and Charles Gounod's *Faust* (1859).

There are occasional traces of *The Lyre* in nineteenth-century
French literature, showing that it was not entirely forgotten,
especially among Sand's own friends. For its effect on Baudelaire the reader is referred to an article by Léon Cellier entitled
"Baudelaire et George Sand" (see Select Bibliography). To me,
the most striking allusion to Sand's work is found in part 3,
chapter 6, of the most famous novel of the century, Flaubert's
Madame Bovary—though the reference would easily escape a
reader who did not know Sand's play. Emma Bovary is thinking aloud and asks, "But if there was somewhere a strong
beautiful being, a valorous nature, full at one and the same
time of exaltation and refinements, the heart of a poet under
the form of an angel, *lyre with brazen strings*, sounding epitha-
lamia toward the sky, why, by chance, could she not find it?"
It is Flaubert's tribute to his friend George Sand and to her
creation.

SAND'S FEMINISM

The significance of Sand's *Lyre* for early nineteenth-century romanticism, and its relationship to some of her own works and
those of others, are perhaps clear from what has been said
above. Obviously the connection between its philosophical
ideas and those of contemporary works, or its musical theory,

could be worked out in greater detail than seemed appropriate here. I do not know what to say about the anti-Semitism of the play; on the one hand, Sand seems to go out of her way to stress the identification of Mephistopheles as a Jew; yet anti-Semitism is also a part of the late medieval atmosphere, inherited from the Faust legend, that hangs over the play, and in that sense the attitude is rather conventional.

The feminism of *The Lyre* is clear from the treatment of the character of Helen, on which some comments have already been made. Beginning in act 1, scene 8, Helen is repeatedly referred to as "daughter of men," suggesting that she may be viewed as a sacrificial figure representing all women. There are doubtless other features of the play that could be discussed in the light of modern feminist criticism. For example, in act 1, scene 8, Helen is identified with the sibyl. The sibyl is a recurring symbol of feminine literary creativity, seen also in the introduction of Mary Shelley's *The Last Man* (1826), as discussed by Sandra M. Gilbert in *The Madwoman in the Attic* (1979). It might be argued that whereas the male characters of the play, including Albertus and the Spirit of the Lyre, take a positive view of historical progress and technology, Helen seems to live and think in space outside of history and with an acute sense of human suffering. Alice A. Jardine's theory of gynesis (*Diacritics* 12 [1982]) could perhaps be applied to *The Lyre*, in the sense that technology and time are here associated with the male, nature and space with the female. (On this see also Julia Kristeva, "Woman's Time," *Signs* 7 [1981].)

In conclusion, and without exaggerating the profundity of *The Lyre*, it seems appropriate to note that some of its themes, often passionately treated, are still significant one hundred and fifty years later. The experience of Helen as a woman is clearly one of these. Especially, perhaps, to an academic, the midlife crisis of Albertus, professor of philosophy, also cuts near the bone. The phenomenon of the scholar who loses confidence in his or her own knowledge and regrets choices of the past is not unknown today. Sand holds out hope that wisdom is attainable. The more general issue of the nature of knowledge still vexes us in the aftermath of the controversy between C. P. Snow and F. R. Leavis over "the two cultures," as it did the nineteenth century in the aftermath of Kant's aesthetic. Does there, in fact, exist a kind of poetic knowledge, complementary to but quite different from scientific knowledge? Sand, again passionately, believed there does, and that it is the more important of the two. Though especially available to a woman, a man may achieve it with effort.

TRANSLATOR'S NOTE

This translation is based on the text of *Les septs cordes de la lyre* in *Oeuvres complètes de George Sand*, new ed., pp. 1–164 (Paris: Michel Lévy Frères, 1869).

Square brackets [ ] indicate supplementary stage directions added by the translator.

 *The Seven Strings of the Lyre*

Eugene, do you remember that sunny day when we heard the son of the Lyre, and when we surprised the seven Spirits of Light leaping in a sacred dance, to the song of the seven Spirits of Harmony? How happy they seemed!
—*Submissive Choruses*, Slavic song, translation by Grzymala
[On the significance of this quotation, see Introduction above.]

Master Albertus [a teacher of philosophy]

Hanz, Carl, and Wilhelm [his students]

Helen [his ward]

Mephistopheles

A Poet

A Painter

A Composer and Conductor

A Critic

The Spirit of the Lyre

Celestial Spirits

Therese, Helen's governess

[Infernal Spirits, Neighbors, Townspeople, et al.]

[The action takes place in a German-speaking university town around 1838.]

 ACT ONE

The Lyre

Scene One

In the study of Master Albertus. He is writing. Wilhelm enters on tip-toe. It is night. In the distance is heard the noise of holiday-makers. [Master Albertus's study is a large room, lined with books. On one wall, a large, full-length window, opening onto a balcony. Against the opposite wall stands a socle, or pedestal, on which rests a highly decorated lyre. Toward the front, a door opening onto a corridor gives access to the rest of the house and to the street; at the back, a fireplace and a small, low bed. In center stage, a large table or desk, covered with books and papers and holding an oil lamp. On each side of the table, chairs.]

ALBERTUS, *without turning his head*: Who is there? Is that you, Helen?

WILHELM, *aside*: Helen! Does she sometimes come to the philosopher's study at midnight?
　(*Aloud*) It's me, Wilhelm. [*He enters; not being invited to sit, he remains standing through the scene.*]

ALBERTUS: I thought you were at the festival?

WILHELM: I've just come from there. I've tried, unsuccessfully, to take up my mind. Usually all I have to do to make my heart thrill with youth and good feeling is to breathe the air of a festival, but today it's different.

ALBERTUS: Don't tell me old age has chilled your blood! That's the fashion everywhere. All young men regard themselves as *blasé*. Still, I wouldn't mind if they were giving up pleasure for study, but it's not a question of that. Their amusement consists in making themselves sad and believing they are unfortunate. Fashion is truly a strange thing.

WILHELM: Master, I admire you. You're never sad or gay. You are always alone and always calm. Public celebration never draws you into its excitement, doesn't make you feel the loneliness of your isolation. You hear the bands pass, you see the buildings illuminated, you even observe the country dancing, with its rainbow colors and the graceful rockets that fall in a shower of gold on the green dome of the big chestnut trees. And there you are, engaged in philosophical speculation on the hypothetical relationship between your peaceful subjectivity and the mad objectivity of all those little feet dancing below on the grass. I don't understand why the white dresses passing and repassing, like ghosts through the greenery, don't give you a thrill, and why your pen runs along the paper as though it were a watchman on his rounds that interrupts the silence of the night.

ALBERTUS: What I feel on seeing a festival can only slightly interest you. But how is it that you, who reproach me with indifference, are come home so early?

WILHELM: Dear Master, I will tell you the truth: I am bored wherever I know I'm not going to meet Helen.

ALBERTUS, *startled*: Do you continue to love her so much?

WILHELM: More all the time. Ever since she recovered her reason through your care she is more appealing than ever. Her past sufferings have left a mark of indescribable languor on her brow; and her melancholy, which discourages Carl and disconcerts even Hanz, is for me a greater attraction. Oh, she *is* charming! You don't notice that, Master Albertus. You see her growing and blooming before your eyes, but you don't know that she is a young woman. You look at her as always a child. You don't even know if she is a blonde or brunette, if she's tall or short!

ALBERTUS: In fact, I think she's neither short nor tall, neither blonde nor brunette.

WILHELM: You've looked at her carefully then!

ALBERTUS: I have seen her often without thinking about looking at her.

WILHELM: Well then, what does she seem to you?

ALBERTUS: Beautiful as a pure and perfect Harmony. If the color of her eyes has not struck me, if I haven't noticed her height, that doesn't mean I am incapable of seeing and comprehending beauty. It is because her beauty is so harmonious, because there is so much accord between her character and her figure, so much unity in all her being, that I experience the charm of her presence without analyzing the qualities of her person.

WILHELM, *a little troubled*: Well said, for a philosopher. I would never have believed you were susceptible . . .

ALBERTUS: Go ahead and make fun of me, my boy. I know you think a philosopher is an offensive and disagreeable animal!

WILHELM: Don't say that, my dear Master. *Mon dieu*, I wouldn't make fun of you!—you, the best and greatest among the best and greatest of men! But if you only knew how happy I am that you don't feel passion for women! — If by some chance you were to perceive too well the graces of Helen, what would become of a poor, beardless student with no brains like myself in competition with a man of your distinction?

ALBERTUS: Dear child, I'm not going to compete with you or anybody. I have too just an estimate of myself. I've passed the age of pleasing and loving.

WILHELM: What are you saying, Master? You're hardly middle-aged! Despite the way you burn the midnight oil in studying, you still don't have a single wrinkle. And when the fire of some noble enthusiasm animates your eyes, young as we are, we lower our gaze as at the appearance of a being superior to us, as at a ray of celestial light!

ALBERTUS: Don't say that, Wilhelm. It distresses me without accomplishing anything. Grace and charm belong exclusively to youth. The beauty of mature age is like an autumn fruit that rots on the branch because the fruits of summer have appeased thirst. (*He pauses.*) To tell the truth, Wilhelm, I never had any youth, and the dried fruit will fall without having attracted the eye or hand of any passersby.

WILHELM: So they have told me, Master, and I haven't been able to believe it. Could it really be true that you have never been loved?

ALBERTUS: Only too true, my friend. But all regret would be vain and useless today.

WILHELM: Never been loved! Poor Master! — But you have known so many other sublimities of which we have no idea.

ALBERTUS, *brusquely*: Yes, doubtless, doubtless. — Wilhelm, do you then want to marry Helen?

WILHELM: Dear Master, you well know it has been my one wish for the last two years.

ALBERTUS: And would you quit your studies to take a job? For eventually you would have to find a way to raise a family. Philosophy is not a lucrative career.

WILHELM: I don't care what I might have to do. As you know, when the question of my marriage to Helen arose, the old lute-maker Meinbaker, her father, demanded that I leave school for his workshop, leave the study of science for instruments of toil, the books of history and metaphysics for the account books of business. The good man wanted as son-in-law only somebody who could work a file and a plane like the most humble artisan and direct his business like himself. Well, I would have signed up for all that: no cost would have been too great to obtain his daughter. I was already capable of assembling the best harp that had left his shop. With the violins, I feared no rival. With God's help, and my little talent and small capital, I could still buy an interest in a business and set up a modest shop in musical instruments.

ALBERTUS: Would you renounce, without regret, the cultivation of your intelligence, the enlargement of the circle of your ideas, the raising of your soul toward the ideal?

WILHELM: You see, Master, I am in love. That's the sum of it. If, back when he was rich, Meinbaker had offered me his immense fortune instead of his charming daughter, and with it the honors which are decreed only to kings, I wouldn't have hesitated to remain faithful to the worship of science, and I would have crushed under foot all material goods to raise myself toward the sky. But for me, Helen is the ideal. She is the sky, or more, she is the harmony that governs celestial things. I have no more need of intelligence. All I need do is see Helen, and right away I understand all the marvels that patient study and the exercise of reason would have revealed to me only one by one. Dear Master, I know you can't understand this, but it's really quite simple. What I believe is that through love I will arrive more quickly at faith, virtue, divinity, than you will by study and abstinence. Otherwise I would not again be resolved to lose my intelligence for the sake of living by my heart.

ALBERTUS: Perhaps your feelings govern you without your knowing it and suggest to you some ingenious sophisms that I don't dare combat for fear you may become infatuated with philosophical pride. Dear child, be happy in your abilities and give in to the force of your youthful impetuosity. A day will certainly come when you will look back, angry at having let your intelligence slumber in these delights . . .

WILHELM: Still, Master, after a career dedicated to scientific speculation, it happens that an austere man looks into the past, angry at having let his passions flicker out in abstinence.

ALBERTUS: You speak too truly, Wilhelm. — Enough, look at this lyre. Do you know what it is?

WILHELM: It is the famous lyre of ivory, invented and assembled by the celebrated lyremaker Adelsfreit, worthy ancestor of Helen Meinbaker. They say he finished it the very day of his death, about a hundred years ago. The good Meinbaker preserved it as a relic, without allowing his own daughter even to breathe on it. It's a precious instrument, Master, and its like is not to be found anywhere. The ornamentation is in such exquisite taste, and the ivory figures all around it of such wonderful workmanship, that admirers have offered immense sums for it. But though financially ruined, Meinbaker preferred to die of starvation rather than to let this incomparable instrument leave his house.

ALBERTUS: Yet this incomparable instrument is mute. It is a work of patience and an object of art which serves no purpose and from which it is impossible to draw any sound. Its strings are loose or rusty, and not even the greatest artist could make it play.

WILHELM: What are you getting at, Master?

ALBERTUS: At this: the soul is a lyre on which all the strings should be played, sometimes together, sometimes one by one, following the laws of harmony and melody. But if you let the strings rust or go slack, though they were once delicate and powerful, it is in vain that you care for the external beauty of the instrument, in vain for the gold and ivory of the lyre to remain pure and bright. The voice of heaven no longer lives in it, and this corpse without a soul is nothing more than a useless piece of furniture.

WILHELM: That can be applied to you and me, dear Master. You have played too much on the golden strings of the lyre, and while you shut yourself up in your favorite subject, the brazen strings are broken. For me the opposite is true. I willingly break the celestial strings that you have touched for the sake of playing with impetuous intoxication on the passionate strings which you hold in too great contempt.

ALBERTUS: And both of us are unskilled, incomplete, blind. One should know how to play with both hands and in all the scales . . .

WILHELM, *without hearing him*: Master Albertus, you have so much influence on Helen's mind! Will you undertake to renew to her my proposals so that she may accept me for her husband?

ALBERTUS: My child, I shall work to that end with all my heart and all my power, for I am persuaded that she could not make a better choice.

WILHELM: Blessings on you, and may heaven crown your efforts with success. Good night, my good Master. Forgive me for being so little philosophical. Forget the ungrateful student who is abandoning you, but remember your devoted friend who will remain always faithful.

Scene Two

ALBERTUS, *alone*: Oh sublime Philosophy! Is it thus that a man deserts thy altars? With what ease thou art forsaken for the first passion that seizes the senses! Is thy empire then really nothing, and thy ascendance really absurd? Alas, how feeble the bonds with which thou enchainest us, since, after years of sacrifice, after half a lifetime consecrated to heroic persever-ance, we feel again, with so great bitterness, the horror of soli-tude and the anguish of ennui!

Sovereign Spirit, Source of all Light and Perfection, thou whom I wished to know, to feel, and to see closer than other men do, thou knowest that I have sacrificed all, and myself more than anything, to relate myself to thee, while purifying myself. Since thou alone knowest the greatness of my sacri-fices and the immensity of my suffering, how is it that thou dost not help me more effectively in my hours of distress? How does it happen that, caught in a dull agony, I consume myself within like a lamp whose light casts a more ardent bril-liance at the moment when the oil is about to give out? How does it happen that instead of being the sage, the stoic, whose serenity everyone admires and envies, I am the most uncer-tain, the most devoured, the most miserable of men?

(*Moving to the balcony*) Eternal First Principle, Soul of the Uni-verse, O Great Spirit, O God! Thou who art resplendent in the sublime firmament and who livest in the infinity of these shin-ing suns and other worlds, thou knowest that it is not love of vain glory or pride in futile knowledge that led me along this path of renouncing earthly things. Thou knowest that, if I have wished to raise myself above other men by virtue, my goal has not been to think more highly of myself than of them, but to bring myself closer to thee, source of all light and of all perfection. I preferred the delights of the soul to the enjoyment of perishable matter; and thou knowest, thou who readest men's hearts, how mine was pure and sincere!

Why then this mortal weakness that seizes me? Why these cruel doubts that tear me? Is the road of wisdom then so rough that the more one advances, the more one meets obstacles and perils? Why, when I have passed victoriously through the passionate years of youth, am I, in my middle age, exposed to more and more terrible trials? Should I then regret, at a time when it is too late, what I scorned when there was still time to possess it? Is the heart of man made so that only pride maintains its force, and the heart would not know how to accept grief if it had not come to it of its own will? They always say that philosophers are full of pride! Perhaps it is true! Perhaps I should have regarded as a pleasant offering to the divinity some privations which it imposed or which it looked on with pity as the condition of our weakness and our blindness! Perhaps I *have* lived without fruit and without merit! Perhaps I have suffered in vain! *Mon dieu!* Sufferings so obstinate, struggles so poignant, nights so desolate, days so long and so dull to carry through to evening!

No! It is impossible, God would not be good, God would not be just, if he did not take account of my great labor. If I have deceived myself, if I have made bad use of my strength, the fault is the imperfection of my nature, the feebleness of my intelligence; and the nobility of my intentions should absolve me!

Absolve me? Nothing more? That is the pardon a judge, in disdainful forbearance, would accord to voluptuaries and egoists! Absolve me? Am I a fanatic, a mystic, who believes God only welcomes to his bosom the ignorant and the "poor in spirit"? Am I a monk who places my faith in a blind master, friend of stupidity and degradation?

No, the divinity I serve is that of Pythagoras and Plato, as well as of Jesus. It is not enough to be humble and charitable to render yourself propitious; it is necessary to be *great*. It is necessary to cultivate the high faculties of intelligence, as well as the gentle instincts of the heart, to enter into commerce with this infinite power, which is perfection itself, which saves in goodness, but which reigns in justice . . . It is by thy example, O Limitless Perfection, that man should make himself just, and justice does not exist without knowledge. If you have not this knowledge, my miserable soul, if your labors and efforts have only brought you to error, if you are not on the path that should serve as the route for other souls, you are cursed, and all that remains is for you to seek refuge in the patience of God, who pardons criminals and relieves the abject . . . The abject! The criminal! I whose virtue terrifies tender hearts and makes envious spirits despair . . . Proud! Proud! It seems to me that from the height of these stars a thunderous voice cries to me: "Thou art nothing but a man of pride!"

O you who live in joy, you whose life is a long holiday, you young whose fresh voices call back and forth from among the trees, where you frolic around the lights like graceful butterflies of the night! Girls beautiful and chaste, who anticipate in innocent pleasure the austere joys of marriage! Artists and poets, whose rule and whose goal is discovery and possession of whatever elates the imagination and delights the senses! Older men, full of projects and desires for positive fulfillment! All you who only form facile plans to be realized, and conceive only naive or vulgar joys! — How contented you all are! But I, alone in the midst of this rapture, I am sad, because I have not put my hopes in you and because you can do nothing for me. You make up together a family of which no part can isolate itself and where each can be useful or agreeable to another. Each one in it is loved or sought by all. There is no one who does not have in his heart some affection, some trust, some sympathy! But I, I consume myself in an eternal tête à tête with myself, with the specter of the man I could have been and that I wanted to kill. Like remorse, like the shadow of a victim, he is bent on following me, and without pause he demands back from me the life I took from him. He scoffs bitterly at the other me, the one I consecrated to the cult of wisdom. And, when he has crushed me with his irony, he finishes me off with his reproaches! Sometimes he returns into me, he winds himself into my breast like a serpent, he breathes there a devouring flame; and when he quits me, he leaves behind a fatal venom that poisons all my thoughts and chills all my aspirations. O children of earth, sons of men! At this hour, none of you is thinking of me, none of you cares about me, none puts hope in me, none suffers for me! And yet I suffer, I suffer what none of you has ever suffered nor will ever suffer. (*The lyre gives a plaintive sound. Albertus remains silent for a few moments.*)

What did I hear? It seemed to me that a voice replied with a harmonious sigh to the sob breathed from my breast. If only it were the voice of Helen! Would my adopted daughter be touched by the secret sadness of her old friend? — Curse the feeble light of this lamp . . . — No, I am alone. Helen is asleep. Perhaps at this moment she is dreaming that, supported on the arm of Wilhelm, she is wandering with him over a mossy park in the moonlight, or that she is dancing there in the grove, beautiful in the brilliance of a hundred torches, surrounded by a hundred young students who admire the lightness of her feet and the suppleness of her movements. Helen is high spirited, she's happy, she's loved. Perhaps she loves in return! She wouldn't know how to think of me! — I, I am forgotten of all, indifferent to all. Who knows? Yes, perhaps! No! That would be shocking! (*The lyre gives a dolorous sound.*)

For once I am not mistaken: there is a voice that chants and cries with me . . . Is it the night wind playing in the jasmines that grow by the window? Is it a voice from heaven that echoes in the strings of the lyre?

No, the lyre is mute. Many generations have passed without awakening the breath now extinct in its entrails. Such a generous heart grows dumb and dries out among unfeeling people who forget it or misunderstand it.

O Lyre, image of my soul, in the hands of a great artist you would have rendered some sounds divine. But as you are now, abandoned, loosened, set on a pedestal to please the eye, like a silly ornament, you are nothing more than an elegant machine, a well-worked case, a cadaver, a learned work of the creator, but a place where the heart no longer beats, and all life has been frightened from you. All right, I shall awaken you from your obstinate slumber. A dead instrument requires the hand of a dead man to play it. (*He approaches the pedestal and takes the lyre in his hands.*)

What am I going to do? What foolish preoccupation seizes me? Even should this lyre, now out of tune, be able to give out sound, my unskilled hand would not know how to apply to it the laws of harmony. Sleep in peace, old relic, masterpiece of an art I do not know. I see in you something more precious, for you are the legacy of a friendship that never failed and the symbol of an adoption whose obligations I shall know how to fulfill. (*He replaces the lyre on the pedestal.*) Let's try to end this distress. (*He seats himself before his desk and for several moments stares into space.*)

How Wilhelm dreams of my ward! What power has love! O fatal passion, he who faces you is courageous; he who denies you is insensitive. Will Helen accept one whom she has already refused? It seems to me that she prefers Hanz. He is more intelligent, but Wilhelm has the more tender heart, and women perhaps take more pleasure in being greatly loved than in being well directed and well advised. Carl also has some feeling of love for her. His is a light head, but he is a very beautiful boy. I suppose that women are themselves light and vain and that a pretty face has more value to them than a noble spirit. Women! What do I know of women? What will be the choice of Helen?[1] What difference does it make to me? I shall advise her what seems to me the best for her happiness, and I will marry her off, in the end, according to her own taste. I only hope that this beautiful and pure creature may not fade under the breath of some brutal lust. —

It's clear I am not getting any work done. My lamp is growing faint. This will have to do as preparation for tomorrow's lecture. Let's try to sleep. When day is here my students will come to call on me. (*He lies down on his pallet.*) Helen does not have much intelligence. She has a just spirit, a right conscience, but her perceptions are limited, and the smallest metaphysical subtlety embarrasses and tires her. Wilhelm will suit her better than Hanz. — I'm giving too much thought to this. It's not the right time.

O God, direct the sentiments of my heart and the functions of my being in accordance with reason and justice. Send me rest. (*He sleeps.*)

Scene Three

Albertus is asleep. Mephistopheles leaps from the last flame as the lamp goes out. [He glows in a reddish luminescence of his own making.]

MEPHISTOPHELES: What dreary, stale employment to keep watch on a philosopher! Really, it seems to me duller than the flame of this lamp, where I was amusing myself by making a

1. Helen is to choose among three suitors, much as Paris, in the classical myth, judged among three goddesses and won Helen as a prize.

silhouette of Helen and her lovers pass on to his paper. These
logicians are distrustful souls. One works like a spider around
their cold brains to catch them in the web of dialectic, but
the result is that they kick and catch the devil in threads of
their own making. They use chicanery to resist the master
who taught it to them! This one uses demonstrative reason
to arrive at faith, and what ruins others saves him from my
claws. You are a mystical pedant who gives me more pain
than did your ancestor, Faust. There must be in your veins
some drops of the blood of the tender Marguerite, for you
want to understand with your heart! I really don't know what
humanity is coming to! Behold, philosophers who want at one
and the same time to understand *and* to feel. If we let them
get away with it, man will slip between our fingers quickly
enough. *Hola*, my masters! Believe and be absurd,[2] we agree
to that; but don't complicate it by trying both to believe and to
be wise. That won't do, for the devil will take a lease on this
wretched plot you're pleased to call your world.

I'll have to take a different tack with you, dear philosopher,
than the fiery approach I used with Doctor Faustus. He had no
lack of violent instincts or pompous egotism; when he was
about to be freed by death, the stupid man lost patience and
regretted not having devoted his life to profit. I knew then
how to rejuvenate him and throw him into the storm. His cold
intelligence would have taken him straight to the truth if I had
not puffed up his passions and aroused in him a flame which
devoured Madame Conscience with a wave of the hand. But
with this one there is fear that his passions may turn to the
advantage of faith. He has more conscience than the other;
pride has taken greater hold of him, vanity none. He has so
trampled indulgence that he is capable of understanding an-

---

2. An echo of *credo quia absurdum est*, "I believe because it is absurd," commonly, but wrongly, attributed to Tertullian.

gelic joy and of saving himself with Marguerite rather than losing her with himself. Thus my business is with your heart, my dear philosopher; when I have killed it, your brain will function by my will. Let's see; let's torment a little this heart so intent on being *sympathique*, and instead of rejuvenating it, let's bury it under the ice of a premature old age. I'll have to start by degrading Helen, or brutalizing her by marriage to a vulture. But the dumb fools will find some way to poetize her domestic virtues. Better would be to debase her by prostituting her to all these philosopher's apprentices who crowd the house from morning to night. As he sees her dirtied, this fine thinker will conceive a horror of youth, beauty, and ignorance. Everything that smacks of romance will seem criminal to him; he will become a complete prude, that's what I'm waiting for . . . Let's go off and find the girl. I have some fine, fiendish reptiles to exercise over her brow while she sleeps. — But there is one obstacle between her and me, and I must destroy it. I was counting on destroying the philosopher by enthusiasm. If I proceed by contraries, I should annihilate the symbol that here lights the flames of the heart. Heh, goblins and fairies, come my brave crooked helpers. Take the lyre and break it to pieces with your claws, reduce it to ashes with your breath. And quickly!

CHOIR OF INFERNAL SPIRITS: Quick, quick! Break the lyre. A spirit rebellious against the sentences of Hell lives in its mysterious breast! A charm holds him in chains. Break his prison so that he can return to his master and will no longer have power to converse with men. Quickly, quickly, break the lyre!

Spirit who was once our brother, and who flatters yourself with being rehabilitated by expiation and with finding a place among celestial powers, you are going to come out of there! Let your master repossess and chain you! You will not purge yourself of your fault by working for the salvation of men. Quickly, quickly, break the lyre!

VOICE OF THE LYRE: Back, Cry of Hell! You have no power against me. A pure hand must deliver me! Accursed! It is in vain for you to arouse against me your legions with their raucous voices. A single celestial note stills all the roar of Hell. Back, and silence!

MEPH.: What do I see! My dreadful legions take flight! This force held in the lyre is stronger than my *liberté*![3]

CHOIR OF CELESTIAL SPIRITS: God allows you to excite others toward evil, but you cannot accomplish it yourself. You cannot move a straw in the universe; you pour your poison into hearts, but you do not know how to make an insect die. Your seed is sterile if man does not render it fertile with his malice, and man is free to conceive a demon or an angel in his breast.

MEPH.: Look, my man is waking up. Let's see if I shall not find some mortal who hates this music as much as the devil and who can aid me in crushing this lyre. (*He flies off.*)

ALBERTUS, *awakening*: I heard celestial music, and marvels of harmony of which I was never sensible were being revealed in my dream. But who, in reality, could reproduce for me such harmony? My mind itself cannot preserve the least trace . . . Yet it seemed at my awakening that I could have sung what I heard. But all that is wiped away, and I hear only the cry of the morning cocks. Day is risen. Let's get back to work, for the students will soon arrive and I am not ready for the lesson. (*A knock at the door*) Already! Every professor ought to have in his house a marriageable daughter. The ardor she gives to the stu-

---

3. Mephistopheles' *liberté* is his freedom of action, retained by the sufferance of God.

dents to visit his house is really wonderful. I don't know if philosophy gains much by it, and if philosophy ought to be very proud of it! (*He goes to open the door.*)

Scene Four

Enter Hanz, Carl, and Wilhelm.

ALBERTUS: Welcome, dear students! I admire your promptness. On other occasions I was often obliged to wake you up, and now you hardly leave me time to sleep.

HANZ: Dear Master, if we have come at a rather early hour without fear of waking you, it is because, while passing under your windows, we heard the sound of music.[4]

ALBERTUS: You are joking, Hanz. Nobody in my house knows anything about music, and you know I am a barbarian in that respect.

WILHELM: That's exactly why we were very surprised to hear a truly remarkable harmony coming from your apartment. We concluded that you had finally consented to have Helen taught music, and that there was some able professor of harp or piano here, although we could not recognize what instrument was producing the enchanting sounds that struck our ears.

ALBERTUS: Are you serious? There is no musical instrument in my house, other than this old lyre of Adelsfreit, and you

---

4. Among Albertus's students, Hanz has the most sensitivity to music and is the most successful at expressing ideas about the arts. As his name suggests, he is partly modeled on Franz Liszt, with whom Sand had had recent conversations about the nature of music, but many of the ideas expressed in the scene are those of Pierre Leroux (see introduction).

know that it is in too poor condition to produce any sound. Yet let me tell you that just now, while I was still sleeping, I too thought I heard a remarkable melody. I attributed the sound to a dream, but I am beginning to believe that some musician has settled near here.

CARL: Perhaps Helen is studying music without your knowledge. I bet she is hiding a guitar under her bed table and plays it while you are asleep. And while I mention it, why do you have the silly idea of so opposing her tastes? It was more than enough that as long as her father was alive this deprivation was imposed on her. The doctors don't know what they're talking about. How can you put any confidence in them?

ALBERTUS: The doctors were right about this, my dear Carl. All nervous excitement was absolutely contraindicated in the young woman's state of neurological disturbance, and all my understanding of mental health led to the same conclusion as their observations of physiological health. The soul and the body equally need quiet to recover that equilibrium which creates health in both cases. You see that my cares have been crowned with prompt success. While a gentle and healthy regime has reestablished the health of this young woman, wise, paternal instruction has brought her spirit to a just appreciation of reality. I have been the physician of her soul, and I had the good fortune to enlighten and fortify this beautiful arrangement. Whichever of you obtains the hand of Helen should see in me a father, and perhaps even something more than that.

WILHELM: Yes, certainly, a guardian angel, a friend with a divine mission. How beautiful it is to accomplish apparent miracles, dear Master.

CARL: Do you really believe, Master Albertus, that Helen has much disposition for metaphysics? She seems to me to be enlightened more by confidence than by conviction. She believes in you with a sort of blindness which is only filial piety; but if she understands philosophy and if your lessons amuse her, I say, "tell it to the Pope."[5]

ALBERTUS: You're talking like a child.

HANZ: Excuse his trivial way of putting it. Let me say something similar in different terms. It isn't that I don't admire you and bless you for having known how, by an entirely moral approach, to bring reason to our dear adoptive sister. But let me engage with you, apropos of her, in a purely speculative discussion. The hour of your lecture has not yet come; we can debate with you for some minutes, for your conversation is always an education and a benefit.

ALBERTUS: My time is yours. I often learn more from hearing you than from responding, for you know many things of which I am ignorant, or have forgotten.

HANZ: Very well, Master. When one is foolish in a certain way I would almost say that it is a mistake to be cured of it. The exaltation of a poetic brain is perhaps preferable to the calmness of cold judgment. Don't you think that Helen was happy when her eyes, animated by the fever, seemed to contemplate the marvels of the invisible world? Oh, yes, then she was still more beautiful, when her gaze was inspired and a strange smile wandered across her half-open mouth, than today with her veiled look and her chaste melancholy. She has become sadder, or at least more serious, to the extent that she has come to feel her heart beat more slowly. Her body can make an effort to respond to material life, but her spirit does not like to descend from the throne it built in the clouds in

5. Literally, "tell it to Rome," a proverbial expression meaning "I'll eat my hat!"

order to become enlightened here below in obscure and painful struggles. What do you think? Do you believe that Helen, in regaining her physical health, has not felt her soul chilled and falling into a dolorous languor? Do you think she doesn't miss her ecstasies, her dreams, and her dances with Titania[6] at the rising of the moon, and her meetings with the king of the gnomes in the resting place of the stars? Which one of us would not give up at least half of his gross, bourgeois health in exchange for the golden visions of poetry?

ALBERTUS: Hanz, you are not speaking according to my values. Are you a poet or an initiate into philosophy? If you are a poet, write your verses, but leave my school. If you are my disciple, don't trouble your fellow students with fantastic reveries and romantic paradoxes. All those inspirations from fever, all those delirious transformations, constitute a purely physical state of illness during which the brain can produce nothing true, nothing useful, and consequently nothing beautiful. I understand and respect poetry; but I accept it only as a clear and bright form, destined to popularize the other truths of science, morality, faith—in a word, philosophy. Every artist who does not set for himself a noble goal, a social goal, falls short in his work. For all I am concerned, he can pass his life in contemplation of the wings of a butterfly or the petals of a rose. I prefer the smallest discovery useful for man, or even a more naive aspiration toward the happiness of humanity. Enthusiasts, according to you, are inspired seers, priests to reveal to us celestial mysteries. Possibly, under the power of a strange enchantment, they may have an overextended sense of the beauty exterior to real things; but if they can find no intelligible language to communicate their enthusiasm to us,

6. Queen of the Fairies in Shakespeare's *A Midsummer Night's Dream.*

such a disturbance of spirit in isolated thought can only be for
them a dangerous state and for others useless.

HANZ: Well, it is time that I tell you frankly, Master, that I am a
poet! And yet I do not write verses and unless you chase me
away I will not abandon you. For I am also a philosopher, and
the study of wisdom only exalts my penchant for poetry. Why
is this true of me, and something else of you? And why is
Helen still different? I can reconcile ideas of order and logic
with the enthusiasm of the arts and the love of dreaming. You,
on the contrary, proscribe dreaming and the arts; for in your
eyes, the one must be converted into laborious meditation,
and the others often succeed in inspiring disorder of thought
and excess of passion. Helen, in her madness, still belonged
to another order of power. She was absorbed into a poetry so
elevated, so mysterious, that she seemed to be in communion
with God himself and not to have any need of the sanctions
imposed by human reason.

ALBERTUS: And what do you want to conclude, boy?

HANZ: Master, let your pupil first recite his lesson to you.
God has thrown us into this crucible of life where, after a previous existence of which we remember nothing, we are condemned to be reduced, reformed, and redistilled by suffering,
by struggles, by doubt, passion, illness, death. We undergo all
these evils for our improvement, for our purification, if I can
so put it, for our perfectioning. From age to age, from race to
race, we make progress slow but certain, and there are striking proofs of this, despite the denial of skeptics. Though all
the imperfections of our nature and all the misfortunes of our
condition tend to frighten and discourage us, all the higher
faculties we have been accorded to comprehend God and to
desire perfection tend to keep us from despair, from misery,
and even from death; for a divine instinct, more and more

clear and powerful, brings us to understand that nothing dies in the universe and that we move on from the milieu where we have sojourned to reappear in a milieu more favorable to our eternal development.

ALBERTUS: That is my faith.

HANZ: And mine too, thanks to you. For the pernicious breath of time, the mockery of false philosophy, the enchantment of the passions, had shaken me and I felt the divine instinct weakened and disturbed in me like a flame which the wind torments. By forceful arguments, by clear logic, by a true notion of the universal history of being, by a profound appreciation of human history, by ardent conviction, founded on the labors of all your admirable life, you have restored my spirit to the truth. By stainless virtue, limitless goodness, a touching sympathy for all creatures who resemble you, whether past or present; by generous patience toward those who deny you or persecute you, you have made yourself master of my heart, and you have reconciled within me the needs of reason and of sentiment. What more do you want from me, Master? If you have a more devoted disciple, more respectful, more affectionate, prefer him to me. The one who best comprehends you is the best among us. Perhaps it is Wilhelm, perhaps Carl. Bless them, but do not speak ill of me, for I love you with all the power of my being.

ALBERTUS: My boy, my boy, do not doubt my tenderness toward you. Doubt more my logic and my science. Now speak . . . you have some ideas.

HANZ: They are these. Humanity is a vast instrument whose strings vibrate under the breath of Providence, and, despite differences in tone, they produce sublime harmony. Many of the strings are broken, many out of tune; but the law of harmony is such that the eternal hum of civilization is raised incessantly from all parts, and all contribute to reestablishing the accord disturbed by the storm which passes . . .

ALBERTUS: Don't you know how to speak except through metaphor? I can't accustom myself to this language.

HANZ: I'll try to adopt yours. We are in agreement about the work of progress, each in his own terms. Each of us thus operates within some structural organization. But each of us affects the actions of others, so that one cannot imagine an individual outside of all the framework of the ideas of his fellows, unless we suppose an individual existing in the void. We are thus all sons of all the men who have preceded us and brothers of all the men who live around us. We are all the same flesh and the same spirit. Moreover, God, who made universal law and variety within uniformity, has wished that just as he has made no two identical petals on a flower, so he would have no two identical human beings, and he has divided the human race into diverse families that we call "types" and among them individuals differ by infinite gradations. One of these families is called the mystics, another the philosophers, another the manufacturers, another the administrators, et cetera. All are necessary, and ought equally to contribute to the progress of man in well-being, in wisdom, in virtue, in harmony. But there is still one type that assumes the grandeur and merit of all the others; for it is inspired, it nurtures itself from them, it assimilates them to it; it transforms them by amplifying them, embellishing them, defying them in some way; in a word, it propagates them and sends them forth over the whole earth, for it is the universal language . . . This family is that of artists and poets. We live from these emotions; we draw them in through all the senses. The coldest spirit, the most austere soul, needs these creations and the gifts of art to feel that life is anything other than an algebraic equation. Yet we treat artists like frivolous accessories of a refined civilization. Reason condemns them, and if they still have permission to breathe, it is because they are necessary to the wise to help them endure ennui and the weariness of their wisdom.

ALBERTUS: Hanz, you speak bitterly. I do not see that the sages of any nation treat artists and poets as pariahs. I don't see that misery or obscurity are their share in society. A dancer, in our age, has the life of a Cleopatra, while a philosopher lives on bitter and coarse bread, between misery and apostasy.

HANZ: Yes, I agree with that. But I could reply that in the name of philosophy an ambitious man holds the highest responsibilities in the state, while, a martyr to his own genius, an artist lives in misery, between despair and vulgarity. I am not envisioning the misfortune of the poet from that point of view. An ambitious poet can do anything he wants in society, just as an ambitious philosopher can, for both can forswear or betray the truth. In the kinds of considerations I am constructing I don't speak of social misfortune or material suffering. I'm looking higher, and not at all concerning myself with individuals; I'm considering the totality of progress that poetry and the arts ought to accomplish. This progress would be most certain, most rapid, most magnificent were it not for the obstinacy of men to repress all risky attempts, to cool all burning inspiration among the poets. I say poets, but I mean all true artists. The present generation is committed to make them walk in tiny steps because, out of vanity at its own little good sense and infatuated with its own little philosophy, it wants its own mediocrity valued by only having mediocre works shown to it. Some people who only understand small actions and small thoughts have created the concept of "realism" for everything that corresponds to their narrowness of intellect and heart. Everything that exceeds that they classify as impossible and absurd. The result is that all great artists work as martyrs to the present for the love of posterity. Unless they have great strength of mind, unless they are remarkable fanatics, they resign themselves to entertaining their contemporaries like tumblers and to depriving the future of the fruits of their genius.

ALBERTUS: You are condemning, son, without knowing it, these artists who are ambitious of glory and who reject the present in order to have in the future a more distinguished place. I grant this sort of ambition exists; it is the most refined. But believe me, if these geniuses had been really obsessed with the importance of their mission on earth, if they had been consumed by the desire to accomplish progress, they would compromise with their pride and would do for love of humanity what they rightly refuse to do for vain riches and vain social distinctions. They would not blush to restrict and reduce their style in order to speak to this vulgar generation in a language intelligible to it, and to inject their grand verities of the future with yeast able to assimilate itself to its grosser substance.

WILHELM: Master, you are forgetting that art is a form, and nothing more. If it is reduced, if it is restricted to the taste of people who do not love beauty and grandeur, it is no longer art, because there is no more beauty or grandeur in the form.

ALBERTUS: You too forget, Wilhelm. Truly, I shouldn't have doubted that I was surrounded by young artists, and I see in this fact the most perfect critique of my poor philosophy.

HANZ: Nothing, Master, is more beautiful than philosophy, but there is something else beautiful too, poetry. Poetry, at one and the same time, is the mother and the daughter of wisdom.

ALBERTUS: Daughter, yes. She ought to recognize that and never make a step without her mother. But I deny that she is mother in her turn.

HANZ: Master, the first man to conceive the thought of God was neither a geometer nor a mathematician nor a philosopher; he was a poet.

ALBERTUS: That's possible. The first man to conceive the thought of God was still uncultured. His spirit could not raise itself to causation through abstraction. His feelings revealed to him an exterior force, superior to his own. Finally, his intelligence confirmed the judgment of his feelings and he no longer invoked them. Poesy became, for all time, the daughter of wisdom.

HANZ: It was not the judgment of the sense that revealed the existence of God to man, it was the instinct of the heart. The flood of sense perception at the contemplation of creation was only accessory to this impulse of the human soul that, thrown upon the earth, felt itself forced also to dream, to desire, to love the ideal. The spirit was still too little exercised in the subtleties of metaphysics to put itself to the trouble of proving the existence of God, but the soul was complete enough and powerful enough to long for God. It divined his existence and felt him, long before caring to define him. This revelation, this first intuition, is poetry, mother of all religion, of all harmony, of all wisdom. To sum up, I define metaphysics thus: "The idea of God"; and poetry is "the perception of God."

ALBERTUS: Your explanation does not displease me, and I agree, with all my soul, dear poet, to your being my father. But I demand that you prove it. Let us see; you instruct me. Open up to me some new idea. Take your flute and play me a waltz. If, meanwhile, there comes to me a solution to the great problems which occupy me, I will believe and be thankful for your preaching, and I will sign myself always, as at the bottom of a New Year's greeting, "your respectful and appreciative son."

HANZ: I can't open up the sky with this cheap flute that you have just discovered in the pocket of my jacket. But if I have only a weak talent, if I possess only a poor grain of poetry, the fault lies with you, Master. For it is you that proscribe the arts from our studies, and we are obliged to play the violin or the clarinet furtively, in cabarets far from your residence. Were it not for the severe indictment that you have brought against music, I would perhaps be a great artist, a poet, a magician like Adelsfreit; and at this very moment I could perform a miracle and convert you. It would be important, believe me; for the great misfortune of poetry is not that it is unrecognized by juries and judges of the *beaux arts*; it is in being ignored by men like you, Master. For just as a great poet holds the future of philosophy in his hands, a great philosopher holds in his the future of poetry. A minister of state can make a hundred mistakes a day, and a faction can plan a hundred intrigues an hour, and the future of poetry will not be shackled at all by the existence of this minister or this faction. But if Albertus is mistaken, the future of poetry may be enslaved for the centuries. Idiots escape with impunity, great spirits do not have the right to err on a single point of human destiny.

ALBERTUS: But still, why do you reproach me? Haven't I always taught that the arts were noble and powerful means to hasten the education of the human race? If I have condemned modern artists as exercising on you, by their mocking frivolity and their bitter skepticism, a pernicious influence, have I not always hailed those great poets in the future who will fit themselves to be the auxiliaries and the propagandists of wisdom?

WILHELM: You believe then, Master, that these poets don't exist today?

ALBERTUS: I am not speaking about particular people. I only say that today poetry has not yet found the word for its providential destiny on earth. There are some productions of art which I admire, because I understand them, because all the world understands them, and because they have a laudable goal . . . You smile, and I know in advance what you are going to say. The works you have seen me approve seem to you vulgar, and their creators don't merit, in your opinion, the title of poet nor that of artist. What is the source of that judgment? Is beauty relative? Is it the result of some conviction? What's beauty to one is not to another?

HANZ: Beauty is infinite. It is a "Jacob's Ladder" that disappears up into the clouds of the sky; every step you climb reveals to you a splendor more shining at the summit. Those who cling to the bottom have only a confused idea of what others, placed higher up, see clearly. But what those higher up see, the others do not comprehend and they refuse to believe it. That is because there are different ways of climbing up this sacred stair. Some clamber slowly and painfully with feet and hands; others have wings and leap up lightly.

ALBERTUS: Always metaphors! You are trying to say that you artists are doves and we logicians sluggish beasts. All right, if the human race is made of those essentially vulgar, while the poets alone, by divine intuition, penetrate to the councils of God, let them reveal it to us, but let them first understand it.

HANZ: They tell it to you through all the voice of art and poetry, but the better they tell it, the less you understand them. For you obstinately close your ears. They have climbed to heaven, they have heard and remembered the concerts of the angels, they translate these for you the best they can;

but their expression always retains something elevated which seems mysterious to you, because your mind-set refuses to go beyond the limits of demonstrative reason. Very well, modify this imperfect mind-set by serious attention to works of art, by study of the arts, and above all by a grand and total commitment to the development and triumph of the arts and of poetry. Philosophy will gain thereby; for I repeat, it is both the daughter and mother of poetry, and if you had never seen the masterpieces of ancient sculpture, you would never have understood Plato.

ALBERTUS: That is because they are really masterpieces. No one denies it. Beauty is there appreciable by everybody.

HANZ: You have seen them without well understanding them. Since their perfection had been consecrated by the admiration of past centuries, you were not put on guard against the natural instinct which was revealing to you, even to you, this perfection. Yet there exist, in centuries less fertile of genius, some men worthy to follow Pheidias.[7] People don't recognize them and people choke them. That's because they are content to cast a glance on the works of Pheidias without believing that it is necessary to study them. Very well, Master. Those who dispense rewards and distinctions created by rulers are, by nature and education, enemies of beauty. The duty of the logician should be to search out beauty everywhere, to discover it, and proclaim it, and crown it. In passing it by with indifference, you do mankind as great disservice as if you allowed a monument of science to perish. All mankind has drunk of beauty. Man's soul must drink of this source of life or it perishes. Human organizations differ: some aspire to the ideal through the spirit, others through the heart, others

7. The most famous Greek sculptor of the fifth century B.C. None of his works survives.

through the senses. If you want human society to be perfected and to arrive at a magnificent equilibrium, it should conceive the ideal equally through the spirit, through the heart, and through the senses, not neglect any of these faculties. Don't hope to lead all men right away to truth by the same means. To those to whom ideal beauty can only manifest itself through the senses, as a preservative against ruin, give the sacred nudity of the Venus de Milo.[8] See your error in that of other moralists who turn with fear from this beautiful material as an unchaste object, likely to trouble the senses. If you understand art, you will know that beauty is chaste, for it is divine. Imagination departs from the earth and mounts to the skies in contemplating the product of celestial inspiration. For this product *is* the ideal.

ALBERTUS: Son, your ideas on this subject seem to me worth thinking about. As a result, those who give themselves to research about the ideal ought, in every way, to work for the perfectioning of their method. Perhaps the crudeness of mind in relation to the arts has led me until now to an error in many respects. But the bell for class has sounded and doubtless all the students are already in the lecture hall. Let's not make them wait. I shall resume this discussion with pleasure. Nothing is more pleasant to me than to be corrected by those to whom I want to provide the ability to understand everything.

HANZ, *embracing him and taking him by the arm to depart*: Excellent Master, truly great soul. (*Wilhelm and Carl follow.*)

WILHELM: What goodness and simplicity!

---

8. Half-naked, armless statue of Aphrodite by an unknown sculptor of around 100 B.C., found on the island of Melos in 1820. First exhibited in Paris in 1821, it is now in the Louvre.

CARL: He is sometimes very strange, but one cannot keep from loving him with all one's heart.

Scene Five

HELEN [*enters alone into the empty room*]: They have left. I am going to arrange my good master's books and papers. O God, what a noble friend you have given me! Why can't I be worthy of him? In return for his care I wish I could please him in all his tastes and satisfy the modest self-love he puts into instructing me. His desire to see me wise is only too clear. But, alas, I have such a limited spirit, so feeble a memory, that I can't make any progress. This long illness has parched my poor head. How painful it is to me to open these big books! The odor of damp parchment makes me faint, and all the letters aligned and printed with discouraging symmetry make me dizzy. The good master's gentleness and patience add to my guilt and remorse. I see clearly that he is distressed by how little honor I do him, but he never expresses the least disappointment. Just yesterday I confused "objectivity" with "subjectivity" and last night I dreamed about the definition of the absolute. I dreamed I was in a beautiful meadow and watched the flow of a stream of living water. It seemed to me that there were some words written in the depths of its transparent bed, and I read there all sorts of beautiful things, as though in a book. I promised myself to recite them to Master Albertus, and I thought he would be pleased with me. But when I woke up, I remembered nothing other than having seen the pure blue sky in very clear and swift running water. O God, why have you given me so vulgar an intelligence? Master Albertus keeps saying, "This will be better tomorrow," but the next day it goes no better than the last. Come—I'm going to study my lesson conscientiously. (*She seats herself at Master Albertus's table and opens a book.*)

When I try to memorize it I understand nothing at all. When he explains things himself, I grasp them, but his old tomes kill me. What barbarous words. Ah, the song of the nightingale. (*She runs to the window.*) No, it is a linnet. What a clear voice! Oh, beautiful modulation! Poor little thing, people haven't taught you anything, but you know much more than I. (*She lets the book fall.*)

How warm the sun is already! It enters here like a stream of powdered gold. I have a sudden desire to gather a beautiful bouquet to decorate Master Albertus's study. He will say "What's this. Did you think of me?" Yet, after all, he does not much like flowers. He casts a glance at them and says "That's very pretty." But he thinks me a cuckoo to look so seriously at the spring flowers. I don't want to put any flowers under his eyes, for yesterday he mentioned hiring me a teacher of botany. Ah, Heavens! If I had to learn all the Greek and Latin names I would not love you so much, my poor little things! O sun! How good it is, and the breeze of the morning . . . Good morning, swallow! Don't be afraid, continue your nest building by the window. Oh dear, if that intimidates you I won't watch you work. How pretty your little feet are! Yet I must close the window and the drapery, for Master Albertus doesn't much like the light of day. He's so accustomed his eyes to work at night . . . But it is too bad not to see the sun's rays on the bookcase. I am going to amuse myself by looking at the lyre, but I won't touch it. My father always got strangely angry when I went close to it. Poor papa! It reminds me of things in a confused way, but of sad things. I don't want to remember. (*She drops a tear. Mephistopheles enters in the figure of an old Jew.*)

Scene Six

MEPHISTOPHELES, *aside*: Quickly, let's try to distract her, for if she touches the lyre, she is lost to us. (*Aloud*) Pardon, my beautiful damoiselle, if I enter here without your permission. I thought to find Master Albertus.

HELEN, *aside*: What a disgusting old man! (*Aloud*) Monsieur, what can I do for you? Master Albertus is in class.

MEPH.: You do not remember me, my dear damoiselle? I had the honor of seeing you often when you were little. I was much involved with your respectable father. Did you not hear him speak sometimes of Jonathas Taer?

HELEN: Certainly, monsieur. He had much business with you. You are a dealer in secondhand goods, I believe?

MEPH.: Precisely. I see you have as much memory as you do grace and beauty.

HELEN: Monsieur, I do not much like compliments, and I assure you I merit none for my memory.

MEPH.: I wager that you recall, however, the last piano that I procured from your father?

HELEN: Alas, yes, monsieur. I had begun to play it when, after three lessons, I fell ill and my father had it carried from my chamber and dismissed my music teacher.

MEPH.: He did rightly. The music would have killed you, delicate as you are. But hear the purpose of my visit today. I have some business to propose to you.

HELEN: To me, monsieur? Please come back when Master Albertus has finished his lecture. He is my guardian.

MEPH.: I prefer to chat with you, for it is a matter which relates only to you. I want to buy your inheritance from you.

HELEN: You are joking, monsieur? I have no inheritance. My father was ruined when he died. All his debts have been paid. Nothing at all has remained for me.

MEPH.: That is very unfortunate!

HELEN: I assure you that it is all the same to me.

MEPH.: I cannot say as much. I have been extremely frustrated in this bankruptcy.

HELEN: There has not been any bankruptcy, monsieur. My father left enough to pay all he owed.

MEPH.: In that case, your guardian should redeem in cash a little matter of five hundred sequins,[9] for which I have a note here. This debt has not been settled.

HELEN: Great heavens! How to do it? There remains nothing. Give me time, monsieur, and I shall work!

MEPH.: You, work? And what do you know how to do, my pretty child?

HELEN: Alas, nothing. But I will learn. I will be brave. Now I see the value of education.

MEPH., *with a half-smile*: You will learn philosophy, eh? Do you know what one gains from philosophy? Rheumatism and eye trouble.

HELEN: Monsieur, you are very cruel.

---

9. Perhaps about $1,000. The sequin was a Venetian gold coin of the later Middle Ages, circulated widely in the East. Here it lends an archaic tone.

MEPH.: Not so cruel as you think, my child. For I come, as I was telling you, to make a business offer. You have an inheritance, whatever you may call it, besides your beautiful eyes and your pretty bust, one which can become a pretty enough capital for business . . .

HELEN: Monsieur, I beg you, spare me your pleasantries. I am not in the mood.

MEPH.: What are you distressed about? Being so pretty, you can find a good match and marry yourself off advantageously. But to the matter at hand: in addition to your beauty and your seventeen years, you have still the lyre of Adelsfreit. It is a precious instrument, however bad state it is in. With some repair, I make myself bold to sell it for at least six hundred sequins. Give it to me, and I will tear up your father's note, and pay you still a hundred sequins for your wardrobe, which is more than modest, from what I see.

HELEN: The lyre? Sell the lyre? *C'est impossible*! My father thought more of it than of his own life. It is the only thing of his that remains to me. You don't know, monsieur, that he had some very unusual ideas about this instrument. He thought it was a talisman, that it brought him good luck.

MEPH.: It did not keep him from being ruined and dying of chagrin.

HELEN: He urged me more than a hundred times never to separate myself from it, whatever happened.

MEPH.: He thought so much of it that when you even started to touch it he went into a wild fury.

HELEN: That's true.

MEPH.: Then one day, curiosity replacing obedience, you dared to bring your hand to it.

HELEN: You bring to mind a memory I had suppressed, and that yet torments me with remorse. The lyre gave a terrible sound . . . I can still hear it.

MEPH.: And your father entered the room at the same instant with a menacing gesture and a furious look.

HELEN: I fell in a faint, and then I have been sick for a very long time and very dangerously, as they tell me.

MEPH.: Oh, you have been mad.

HELEN: Mad! What do you mean by that? That's outrageous. No one has ever called me mad.

MEPH.: I apologize if I have shown a lack of gallantry. But it's not surprising that you should be insane. Monsieur your father was mad.

HELEN: That's not true. You are a liar and an impostor.

MEPH.: Ask Master Albertus, Wilhelm, whom you have refused to marry, Hanz, who is sweet on you . . . and Carl, who perhaps is not displeasing to you.

HELEN: You are insolent.

MEPH.: Don't get upset. Your father was a monomaniac, that's all. Very sensible in other ways, but he made extravagant claims about his ancestor Adelsfreit, whom he believed a sorcerer, and about his lyre, which he thought bewitched. The fact is that he gave you such a fine fright the day he surprised you scraping the strings of the poor instrument that you fell into a brain fever. It is the nature of these maladies to start up again when the causes are present that gave them birth. That's why Master Albertus has forbidden you to touch the lyre. If he were more prudent he would have hidden it, for you only have to have the fantasy of touching it again, and this time you will be mad for life. That would be annoying to him, for you couldn't get married, and you would remain in his charge. The dear man isn't rich. He is forced, by lack of money as by his love of philosophy, to wear rather worn clothes, and his food is as meager as his person.

HELEN, *drawing back from the lyre with fright*: Oh, yes. Albertus lives with privation, and as for me, I lack nothing. It's the truth. Have I not continually worried about the expense I occasion him? I think of nothing else but myself . . . Ah, I would marry anybody to disembarrass him of me.

MEPH.: My advice is to take Carl. He's got the most style, the most money, and the least pedantry of the three. But that's none of my business, you will say. For the rest, your guardian loves you so much that he could marry you himself, although he is old enough to be your father. It's true that if he has children he will have to ask for charity . . . But when one loves, all is happiness and poetry, *n'est-ce pas?*

HELEN: All that you say is bitter as bile. I would prefer to become a beggar myself rather than increase the misery of my honorable friend.

MEPH.: He will still have to become a little more miserable, for I need my money. Tomorrow I want to leave for Venice and tonight I must complete collecting my capital. You don't want to sell me the lyre?

HELEN: *Mon dieu, mon dieu!*

MEPH.: Stop, you're right. Oh, don't trouble yourself. There's enough here to pay me. The furniture will do well enough.

HELEN: But nothing here belongs to me. You don't have the right to seize my guardian's property.

MEPH.: But I do have the right to send you to prison. And as your guardian does not want to let you go there, and as he has no money, it will be necessary for him to sell his furniture and effects. Bah! There's a good coat hanging on the wall. It's rather too good for a philosopher. A philosopher shouldn't fear the cold. And his bed—why it's quite voluptuous. A pallet ought to do for a stoic.

HELEN, *throwing herself on her knees*: Oh, don't deprive him, don't make him suffer. He isn't young; he is often ill, and he already imposes too many privations on himself. Have me taken to prison, as long as he doesn't know . . .

MEPH.: What good will it do me for you to be in prison? The only advantage to me is to get the debt paid by your guardian. Let's get going. I am going to send my agent to him now, for I don't have an instant to lose. I have ten similar affairs to finish today.

HELEN: Oh, sir, wait until Master Albertus returns. I will tell him to sell you the lyre.

MEPH.: He'll never want to. Master Meinbaker entrusted it to him on deposit. It's all your fortune. He would rather sell his bed. I would do the same in his position. When one has so pretty a ward . . .

HELEN, *standing up*: Be silent, monster, and take the lyre. It's yours. Give me that note.

MEPH.: Not so fast! I can't take the lyre myself. You would think I was taking more than my due.

HELEN: What difference does it make to me? Take what you can. Since I have to lose it, take it *tout de suite*.

MEPH., *aside*: Damn that magic charm! I am forbidden to touch the lyre myself. I have to have it carried by my dupes. (*Aloud*)

No, mademoiselle, that's not how I conduct my business. It's a point of honor with me. I've already contracted sale of the lyre, but I want the sale to be concluded in your presence. The persons who wish to acquire it are just two steps away. I will run to get them. Remember that if you gain anything in return you can use it to lessen the misery of Master Albertus. (*He leaves.*)

HELEN, *alone*: He is right. How comes it that such an avaricious and disgusting man has a kind of delicacy? Mad! I have been out of my mind. Perhaps I still am! Yes, that's why I cannot learn anything and why I am as simple and limited as a child. That is also the reason why I cannot feel love for anyone and decide to marry. If I am insane, it follows that I do well not to put myself as an invalid in charge of a husband. And I ought not to be a mother, for insanity is hereditary . . . But am I then going to remain in the charge of Master Albertus? What a weight on him! Too generous friend! How unfortunate I am! I will kill myself. It is necessary. This wicked Jew has shown me all my misfortunes.

Scene Seven

[*The same. Enter*] *Mephistopheles, the Composer, the Poet, the Painter, and the Critic.*

MEPHISTOPHELES, *aside on entering*: Come, my hearties, if you don't break the lyre, if you don't skin it, if you don't throw it piece by piece into a swamp, I'll never again feel at home among thieves and rogues.

(*Aloud, bowing to the ground before them*) Enter, noble gentlemen. Right here, my illustrious scholars. Let your honors deign to cast an eye on this marvel of art, without forgetting as well (*pointing to Helen and lowering his voice*) to cast a look on this marvel of nature.

HELEN, *aside*: What unpleasant figures. To think my father's treasure is going to pass into their hands. I will not be present at this sale. It would hurt me too much. (*She leaves.*)

COMPOSER: I intend, above all, to try this incomparable instrument. They say it has so marvelous a quality of sound. I plan to introduce it into His Majesty's orchestra. I have already composed a solo expressly for it in my symphony in D major.

PAINTER: I fear you have been deceived. They tell me that no one has heard the sound of this lyre, because the owner would not allow it to be touched. But my friend Lottenwald has told me of the ivory figures which encircle the instrument. He said they were the most beautiful figures of sirens that he had ever seen.

POET: Lottenwald knows what he's talking about. As for me, I plan to put in verse the fantastic legend which belongs to the lyre of Adelsfreit. They assure me, Master Jonathas, that you alone know the true version. It is said to be a very curious tradition, and that the late lutemaker Meinbaker told it only to his best friends, and then under seal of an inviolable secret. I had hoped, because of my position as court poet, to have enough right to consideration that he would confide this mysterious history to me, but he never wished to lend himself to it.

PAINTER: Because you planned to tell it to the public under seal of an inviolable secret. As for me, my demands are less. I would like to copy the figures in order to decorate the frames of portraits of the imperial family. His Majesty is well aware of this invention. He particularly likes the frames of pictures. One could say that he deigns to prefer them to the pictures themselves.[10] This is what I particularly look for in the choice of paintings which he has charged me to collect for his gallery.

COMPOSER: Shut up, you unpleasant person. What does it matter if His Majesty understands the arts as long as he encourages them?

MEPH. (*He shows them the lyre on its pedestal.*): *Voilà*, messieurs, this admirable instrument! As you say, they have not deceived you. Its like does not exist in the world.

COMPOSER: Ah, is that it? I was expecting something different.

PAINTER: I beg a thousand pardons, monsieur Jonathas, but I know a little about this kind of instrument. That is not an Adelsfreit.

MEPH.: How is that, monsieur! Just cast your eyes on the sound box, where you can read the full name of the famous lutemaker and the date . . . the authentic date, the year of his death.

PAINTER: And the distinctive mark you mentioned to me?

MEPH.: Here, engraved in silver on the ebony of the box.

COMPOSER: These are unreadable characters.

---

10. This and the previous sentence are among the "five or six phrases too risky" (Sand, *Correspondance*, 4, no. 1843) that Buloz did not want to publish. They refer to the notoriously bourgeois taste of Louis-Philippe and his picture collection at Versailles. Sand may have had in mind a passage from Rousseau in which he recommended simple frames for good pictures: "It would be a pity if the frame distracted attention the object merits" (*Emile* [Paris: Garnier-Flammarion, 1966], book 2, p. 184).

CRITIC: Ah, good. I will read them right off. I have the eye of a lynx. Listen, listen:

> He who keeps my virginity
>   Shall have riches;
> He who makes me speak well
>   Shall have wisdom;
> Whoever violates me,
>   Will go mad;
> And if he breaks me, he will pay
>   With his life.

POET: Enough of that. It means nothing.

PAINTER: There is some local color in those verses. But frankly, what do you think of the carved figures?

POET: Admirable, sublime!

COMPOSER: And the ornamentation! What exquisite taste! What delicacy in the garlands of flowers! What elegant clusters of leaves! What playful and subtly drawn arabesques! It's a jewel!

PAINTER: I regret not sharing your enthusiasm. All this is trivial, mannered, in bad taste. It's pure rococo. We do better than that today.

CRITIC: I doubt it. Today people make nothing that lasts, and this is a *chef-d'oeuvre*.

PAINTER: In admiring it you put yourself at ease. One is not jealous of the dead.

POET: My friend, one cannot deny that your art is in full decadence . . .

PAINTER: I swear I haven't read a single verse as good as this one for ten years.

COMPOSER: The verse is not bad; I shall put it to music. But I will keep from accompanying it on an instrument of this sort. The construction is detestable, and music, today, is too intellectual, too extended, too complicated to be executed on a kettle like this.

CRITIC: Music, painting, and poetry are buried in the same tomb, my dear friends. There remains only one faculty, criticism.

PAINTER: And on what does it operate? What does this faculty govern? If there is no more art, there is nothing to criticize, and criticism can stretch out on top of our tomb, like a dog on the corpse of its master.[11] Let's see, honestly, to what it is applied.

CRITIC: It is used to write epitaphs.

PAINTER: That is to say you are in the business of an undertaker. It doesn't matter to me, my friend. Go ahead and throw flowers on my tomb. I've always admitted that the barbs of critics bring honor to artists. Meanwhile, be so good as to hold the lyre a little,—like that—. Very good. I'm going to make a quick sketch of the figures while you discuss the price with Master Jonathas. As for me, I'm not buying.

CRITIC: Do you want to copy them, seeing they are so bad? Really, the moderns are very kind to take from the ancients, considering that they are so superior to this second-rate, rococo art.

MEPH., *aside*: I am not going to push for the sale. It's good to let them get heated up in conversation. Within ten minutes

11. Compare Jean-Paul Sartre's comment that most critics have found a small, tranquil place in the cemetery (*Qu'est-ce que la littérature?* [Paris: Gallimard, 1948], p. 37).

they're going to be arguing. If they can break up the lyre without leaving here, that would be the quickest and surest.

PAINTER: Hold still. A little to the right. Good! That's right.

CRITIC: This head of a muse at the top, toward which the sirens bend with such grace, is worthy of antiquity.

COMPOSER: Is it Polymnia or Saint Cecilia?[12]

POET: It is Erato. The lyre is much more the emblem of poetry than of music.

COMPOSER: What pretense! Try to make an instrument sound by reciting verse! Your sonnets wouldn't even move an old fiddle—my dear friend.

POET: To the ancients the lyre was only an accessory, an accompaniment to declamation, a means of supporting the voice and of marking the verse in a certain measure. For example, wait . . .

COMPOSER, *laughing*: Ah, good. Are you going to play the lyre now?

POET: Why not? All that's needed is to know the intervals of the strings and to follow poetic rhythm. Listen!

MEPH., *aside*: O Lyre, behold your end! (*The Poet declaims some verses while touching the strings of the lyre, which remains mute.*) Damn the rebellious spirit that won't speak!

CRITIC, *softly, to Painter*: That's the worst that he's done yet.

POET: Well, what do you say to that?

---

12. Polymnia (or Polyhymnia) is an unlikely choice, since she was usually regarded as muse of the mime; Saint Cecilia was patron saint of musicians; Erato was the muse of lyric poetry, and, as the Poet says below, it is she who was intended.

COMPOSER: The verses are beautiful.

POET: And the accompaniment? You wouldn't have thought me capable of such accompaniment?[13]

COMPOSER: What accompaniment?

PAINTER: You wiggled your fingers with lots of grace!

COMPOSER, *to Critic*: Did you hear an accompaniment?

CRITIC: The gentleman accompanied himself with fine gestures, a very noble pose, and a truly remarkable expression on his face.

POET: Sir, you try in vain to make me seem ridiculous. I am not a musician. My profession is more elevated. If I have drawn from this lyre some harmonious sounds, all the credit for it goes to the skilled workman who made it.

COMPOSER: But, my friend, it's you who would amuse yourself at our expense. I give you my word of honor that you did not draw any sort of sound from this instrument.

POET: I find you amusing too. Imagine a deaf composer! That explains your symphonies.

CRITIC, *to the Composer*: Don't argue with the man. It's one of the most beautiful privileges of poetry to see and hear in darkness and silence.

PAINTER, *still sketching*: As for me, I was so ravished and absorbed by the gentleman's verses that I didn't even notice the accompaniment.

POET: I am not looking for praise. I only want to make you admit the beauty of the sounds I drew from this lyre. Wait! Is

13. The poet imagines he has heard the music inherent in his verses, but no one else hears it.

there anything more pure and more powerful than this chord?
(*He touches the lyre, which remains mute.*)

COMPOSER: You see?

PAINTER: Did you hear anything?

CRITIC: *Rien du tout!*

POET: You are all rather nasty. I am crazy to let myself be
conned. I'll play for myself alone. (*He plays while speaking.*)
What sonority! What a celestial harmony! But that's strange!
The sounds produce themselves and begin, miraculously, to
vibrate under my fingers. Listen! What purity in my playing, what lightness of touch in the arpeggios, what a power
in these sublime chords! O poetry, Queen of the Universe, to
you I owe a talent I know not, which I regard as secondary,
and which by the power of my genius raises itself to the
sky! The rest of you stand mute, astonished, frightened, con-
founded by my playing. Miserable hacks, it would take you
ten years of study to be good enough to perform in a mediocre
way on a shepherd's pipe. But without ever having learned
music, without knowing the rules of the art or the technique
of any instrument, I unfold here, without effort, without care,
without meditation, the treasures of my soul. Almost involuntarily, I make torrents of harmony trill forth. I see everything around me come to life. These columns dance, the
ceiling undulates, and the walls open up to let the glorious
hymns which breathe from me rise up to the empyrean heav-
en. (*The lyre remains silent.*)

COMPOSER: What a shame! Our poor friend has gone mad.
Who will write my librettos now?

CRITIC, *with irony*: I don't find the gentleman any madder
than usual.

PAINTER (*He laughs suddenly and turns around on his chair.*): I'm dying, I'm suffocating. I've never seen anything so amusing!

POET: *You* excite *my* irony and my pity. Your jealousy is evident, and at the moment when my force bursts forth, your hate of everyone cannot contain itself. You've always been my enemies, I know it. Go to hell! And if I listened patiently to your flattery, it is because my misunderstanding was saving you from my indignation. But it's time I left this impure atmosphere. I separate myself from you. I am going to fill the world with my glory, and like the divine Orpheus bring to men the benefits of civilization in the sacred language in which I stole the secret from the gods! (*He takes himself off through the balcony, his hat in hand.*)

MEPH., *aside*: Curses on you, bird-brain. Look, he takes his hat for the lyre. Let's let these others quarrel a bit. (*He withdraws by himself.*)

PAINTER, *still laughing in bursts*: Look at him, look at him! What a theatrical exit! What contortions! His hair disheveled, his coat flapping in the breeze, his hat in his hands as if it were the harp of Ossian![14] Perfect, perfect! What an excellent creature!

COMPOSER: You laugh, but he is mad, really mad! It's an attack of brain fever.

PAINTER: Bah! It's only an attack of insane vanity. He's used to this malady. He won't die of it.

COMPOSER: But what extravagances he makes! Look how he bows and gives blessing around himself as though he saw a

14. Ancient Irish bard. James Macpherson's *Poems of Ossian* (1760–62), allegedly translations of Gaelic originals, enjoyed great popularity with the early romantics.

crowd at his feet! There, he's climbing on an orange crate and posing like a statue on a pedestal.

CRITIC: Behold Apollo! It's all very well. The hat represents the lyre quite nicely. I bet he imagines the queue of his wig to be the tail of a comet.

COMPOSER: I don't find it laughable. This lyre is bewitched.

"Whoever violates me
   will go mad."

That's a prediction now realized.

CRITIC: It doesn't require much sorcery to predict that a fool will be foolish, and I swear to you that all the machinations of hell could not add anything to the extravagance of a man so content with himself.

PAINTER: It doesn't matter. I must hurry to complete this sketch. Cursed idiot who interrupted me!

COMPOSER: While the Jew isn't paying attention, I want to take down the lyre to examine its interior mechanism. That would determine whether I buy it.

MEPH., *aside*: Yes, yes, be my guest, I ask nothing more. (*The Composer takes the lyre.*)

PAINTER: Ah, I beg, an instant . . .

COMPOSER: Why are you amusing yourself with that, my dear Painter. Don't waste your time when you could do something else.

PAINTER: What's that you say? Don't you see my two sirens? I think I have caught the curve with the feeling of the thing.

CRITIC: Naughty, naughty! Your two satyrs aren't bad, but I prefer the sirens. Why, for that matter, are there satyrs on such an instrument?

PAINTER: There you have the true manner of the critic. He's asked to judge a heroic poem and when he despairs of finding anything there to snipe at he sharpens his pen and writes as follows: "As to the poem as a whole, it contains certainly some beauties; but if we consider it as we ought and as we wish to consider it under the general rubric of geometry and the natural sciences, we are forced to classify it below all that is most mediocre in this genre," etc. etc. (*To the Composer*) That's how it is, right?

COMPOSER: Of what do you speak? Of the critic or of your drawing?

PAINTER: Forget criticism. I'm making fun of it. As to my sirens, ah!

COMPOSER: And your satyrs?

PAINTER: You too? All right, bear up! All the same, they are perfect!

CRITIC: You have the fancy to make some satyrs in place of sirens. There is no point in discussing the fantasy of an artist. But as to what truly relates to the lyre, how would you pretend to copy it? You are not imitating only the shape.

COMPOSER: Doubtless. In place of these two figures, so supple and inclined one toward the other with so much grace, you twist backwards two grotesque trunks and you arrange them on a plan entirely the reverse of the model. It's possible there is some originality there, but I don't see any resemblance to the lyre of Adelsfreit.

PAINTER: Dear maestro, you are too dense to grasp the spirit. Be content to rob some great masters and give us as the inspiration of your muse some disgraceful sounds badly disguised under a decoration of bad taste. Leave light irony to this man who makes such good use of it, as everybody knows, and whose anathemas are, for men like me, certificates of immortality. (*To the Critic*) Yes, monsieur, I defy you and hold you in contempt. You know it well. In looking at this simple sketch, filled with a grandeur that you do not know how to appreciate, you grow pale with rage. And being unable to understand either the beauty or the grace, you affect to see some grotesque subjects in these charming emblems of seduction . . .

CRITIC, *to Composer*: Emblems of seduction! Two hideous satyrs, full of wine and betraying themselves with an obscene laugh!

COMPOSER, *to Painter*: On my honor, sir, your eye is confused or your spirit troubled. These two goat-footed men are unworthy of you. Get a hold of yourself, I beg you. Open your eyes, and don't be offended at my advice—given in your own interests—to destroy the sketch.

CRITIC: That's my advice too.

MEPH., *aside*: Keep at it. Slug away.

PAINTER, *in anger*: So that's the way you want it. My "good" friends, I know you well. You've betrayed me so many times that I have learned to treat your advice as it deserves. Miserable imitators that you are, you look with jealousy at the growth of anybody else's talent. You want to erase all superiority and, accustomed as you are to copy in a servile way, you cry out "bizarre" and "exaggerated" when, in imitation of a work of art, you see the genius of an artist surpass his model. Right you are, my two sirens do not at all resemble those of the lyre, any more than your works, put side by side, resemble the works you have imitated. But there is this difference. You grossly besmirch everything you touch, while I give a sublime imprint to the copy of a subject modest in itself. The sirens of this lyre are two pretty girls, mine are two goddesses, and your efforts are vain. Posterity will judge and confound your jealousy and blind stupidity. (*He leaves, carrying his portfolio with him.*)

COMPOSER: This gets weirder and weirder. He, too, is overcome with dizziness and becomes mad for having only looked at this lyre. The prediction is realized. The delirium of vanity seizes mediocre talents that violate the virginity of the magical object. O magic lyre, I recognize the supernatural force that resides within you, and since you promise wisdom and prosperity to one who makes you speak worthily, I approach you with a respectful confidence and venture the hope of drawing from you harmonies so that all the powers of heaven and hell that presided at your formation will come to submit themselves to me and obey me as if I were great Adelsfreit himself.

CRITIC: Be careful. Everything that happened before our eyes shows something unusual at work and should serve you warning . . .

COMPOSER: You doubt my powers?

CRITIC: Yes, I doubt them, I tell you. I have praised you enough in public, have rendered you enough service for you to have a little confidence in me. Be content with the crowns my good will has brought you. Be content with the renown my pen has conferred. You have abused men; don't play with spirits of another order.

COMPOSER: I don't know what you mean, and I'm afraid that having put a profane hand on the lyre you have lost the spirit. I owe my renown only to my masterpieces, and the venal pen of a scribbler can't bestow crowns. Genius crowns itself. It gathers laurels with its own hands, and it holds in contempt the self-interested advice of flatterers who want to cast doubt on its force to give themselves some importance.

CRITIC, *holding out the lyre to him*: You're the one who wants it. So be it. Let your insensitive rashness bear its fruit and let your destiny be fulfilled.

COMPOSER: On your knees, valet!

MEPH.: Ah, this time, lyre, you are ruined!

COMPOSER (*He takes the lyre and draws from it some sharp and discordant sounds.*): That's strange. Silent! Silent for me as for the poet.

CRITIC: You call that silence? Rain from heaven! You've made my ears bleed.

PAINTER, *returning with the Poet*: What a terrible cacophony! Ah, I see it's you, dear maestro, who gives us this diabolic concert. My astonishment is over.

POET, *holding the Painter's album half-open*: I've never experienced anything so disagreeable as hearing this awful screeching, unless it is seeing these monstrous satyrs grinning at the lewd comic mask of Silenus[15] placed between them, where there should be the ravishing head of the muse that surmounts the lyre.

---

15. Silenus, in Greek art, usually has the features of a horse, whereas satyrs have those of a goat. Silenus is often presented as old and drunk; satyrs are young, and their predominant characteristic is lechery.

PAINTER: In saying that, my good friend, you are staring amorously at the corner of your hat, which you persist in mistaking for the lyre of Orpheus.

COMPOSER: The infernál powers are against me. I call upon you, O Heavenly Spirits! Come give life to this captive harmony! Make it come to life under my fingers. And at the creative breath of my intelligence, let it rise in sounds divine! (*He touches the lyre. It replies in sounds more and more discordant and unendurable, which he doesn't hear.*)

PAINTER: For the love of God, stop. You are setting our teeth on edge.

POET: What abominable noise. It's like a cat fight on the roof, or a witches' sabbath in full flight.[16]

COMPOSER: Still crazy? I tell you, if I haven't made the lyre speak, at least I have not violated it. The madness hasn't come on *me* and *I* am not imagining hearing celestial music coming from this mute instrument.

POET: You mean you don't hear the sharp false chords that shriek and screech and cry under your fingers? If you're not crazy you must be deaf. I told you rightly. You don't hear my divine accords and neither do you hear the terrible clamor you're making.

PAINTER [*at the window*]: Stop, stop! Professor Albertus's lecture has been interrupted. Look down there! The students are looking around in terror and the neighbors are trying to get away in all directions from such a detestable ringing. Should I announce that it is the opening of your new symphony?

---

16. "Witches' sabbath" is perhaps an echo of the Walpurgis Night scene in Goethe's *Faust* (part 1, lines 3835–4220). Compare also the cacophonous music of hell in Gautier's *Albertus*, stanzas 115–17.

COMPOSER: I'm not replying to the insults of a madman. But I was insane myself to have believed that this rotten instrument held a magic power. I see now that it has nothing marvelous, and the reason it won't play is that the sound box is cracked and the strings are rusty. There's nothing here that isn't quite natural. The greatest genius in the world couldn't make a piece of wood speak, and even the most valid contradiction is enough to crack open the heads of people lost in their own vanity. That's why the lyre is mute and that's why you are all fools.

MEPH., *aside*: I'm beginning to think that the devil himself is going mad. What was I thinking of when I counted on these idiots to help me in some way? The Spirit of the Lyre mocks them.

CRITIC, *to Composer*: Make an exception in my case, monsieur. I have watched serenely and impartially your various attempts to discover in this lyre some trace of the glorious genius of our fathers. I have seen here a poet trying to touch mute strings and persuading himself that he pours upon us torrents of harmony. It is the result of impotence joined to inordinate pride. I've seen a painter straining to grasp at least the form of art, and instead of a conscientious and patient study, producing a monstrous fantasy that he believes contains some ineffable grace. That is again impotence joined to blind vanity. Finally, I have seen a composer who produces at random some shrill sounds and an insupportable dissonance. Accustomed as he is to mistake melody and surprise the senses by a confusion of instruments whose noise he takes for harmony, he has lost all his sense of hearing and does not himself suffer at his execrable aberrations. That is still the result of impotence without remedy, joined to gross self-confidence. It is a sad spectacle for one who, like me, holds the balance of criticism, to see so much miserable failure and shameful perversion. This grievous experience confirms us in the conviction, painful but irrevocable, that inspiration does not exist and that our fathers took to their graves all the secrets of genius. There remains for us nothing more than laborious study and austere and persevering examination of the means by which they clothed in irreproachable form the creations of their creative intelligence. Work on, O artists. Work without release, and in place of idly tormenting your decadent imagination in producing monstrosities, apply yourselves to sorting out, at least, in pure and regular lines, the eternal types of beauty and truth which belong not to new generations to change. Since Homer, all attempt at invention has only served to signal the incessant and fatal process of inevitable decadence. You who want to handle the sistrum and the lyre, study rhythm and confine yourselves to style. Style is everything. And invention is nothing, because invention is no longer possible.

PAINTER: There you have a fine discourse. "But turn again, pray, and someone will reply."[17]

POET: You basely insult us. Impotent in thought, because impotent by nature, you accuse us of impotence because you hope to discourage us and make us descend to your level.[18] All right, prove, if you can, that you're capable of producing something—anything at all. Just make us a passable verse to prove you've studied the form. I defy you to do it!

PAINTER: Just trace a line with this pencil.

---

17. *Mais tournez-vous, de grâce, et l'on vous répondra.* Since this alexandrine line is spoken by the painter, not the poet, one might expect it to be a quotation, but extensive search of dramatic poetry known to Sand has not turned up its source. Possibly it comes from some now-forgotten play of the time.

18. This could be read as a jibe at Prosper Mérimée, who spent one unsuccessful night with Sand and said nasty things about her afterward (see Maurois, *Lélia*, pp. 153–54).

COMPOSER: Just make a chord sound on this lyre. That's what I'm waiting for.

CRITIC: Empty clouds of glory to me lack perfume. I take my refuge on the summits of immutable equity, where I am nourished by serious and lasting joys. I scorn the futile toys you call your scepters and your crowns. I leave them for you to pick up. If I had wanted, I too could have played with ephemeral glory and shone with frivolous glitter. I preferred to be your adviser, your buttress, your teacher in everything. Unteachable students, take care! If you don't pay attention to my lessons, I shall know how to unmask you and to keep you from misleading the age.

PAINTER: One lesson, one little lesson in painting, I beg of you. Wait, here is my pencil. Draw a hand, a foot, a nose, whatever you want.

POET: Improvise a stanza of verse, come on. That we may at last see what you know how to do.

COMPOSER: No, let him play the lyre and if he can, we'll render him homage.

PAINTER AND POET: I agree. Get on with it.

CRITIC, *taking the lyre*: All right, I consent to show you that I know better than you the arts you profess. I am going to recite, in alexandrine verse, a dissertation on painting, and I'll accompany myself on the lyre in the Ionic mode.[19]

PAINTER: That will be splendid and truly new. Let's see you do it.

THE OTHERS: Let's see! Begin!

---

19. One of the fifteen tones of Greek music, commencing on the note B.

MEPH., *aside*: Get on with it, you! You're the one I'm counting on.

(*The Critic puts his fingers on the lyre and withdraws them with a cry of pain.*)

THE OTHERS: What is it? What's happened to you?

MEPH., *aside*: Spirit of the Lyre, you triumph!

CRITIC: Villains! You didn't tell me that the strings were as sharp as the blade of a dagger. I've cut myself to the bone.[20] Ah! My blood is flowing in torrents, and a burning sensation spreads to all my limbs. I'm dying! Help me!

COMPOSER: He's turning pale. His wound is bleeding horribly! It's a punishment from heaven!

POET: He's going to die. Divine justice shows itself at last and confounds the rage of envy!

PAINTER: I pray the source of his impure blood be dried up forever and not give life to a new race of monsters.[21]

CRITIC, *with fury*: Detestable criminals! This is betrayal! You've set this trap to get rid of me, your judge and master. But you will not rejoice for long in your triumph. Before dying, I will break your lyre and no one after me will use it. (*He takes the lyre and tries to smash it. Hanz enters suddenly and snatches the lyre from him.*)

HANZ [*rushing into the room*]: Stop! You are wicked guests and deserve to be thrown out of here. You know the inestimable value Master Albertus attaches to this instrument, and

20. The critic, with his sharp wit, is used to cutting others to the bone.
21. In classical myth, the Furies were born from drops of blood that fertilized the earth at the castration of Uranos.

not content with touching it without his permission, you still want to destroy it. Get out, unfeeling wretches, or I'll draw down on you the anger of Master Albertus and all his school. See, they're all coming now. Leave quickly, or I'm not responsible for what may happen.

(*The Critic, Composer, Painter, and Poet withdraw.*)

MEPH., *aside*: Damned student! I'll make you pay for your fine zeal. I've got to disappear, for the figure of the Jew Jonathas shouldn't be seen too closely by these rascals. (*He flies out the window.*)

Scene Eight

[*Enter Albertus, Carl, Wilhelm, and Helen.*]

ALBERTUS: Is it you, Hanz, who interrupts the lesson with this hubbub?

HANZ: Far from it. My eardrums are still ringing.

CARL: Not even on Mardi Gras have I heard more grotesque horns.

WILHELM: Say rather it was the trumpet of the Last Judgment.

ALBERTUS: But who permitted it, in my house, this wicked foolishness? Does the lyre of Adelsfreit make such sounds?

HELEN, *in a sort of bewilderment*: The lyre has been violated and the lyre has taken its vengeance. It has punished its profaners. The first part of the prediction of my ancestor Adelsfreit has been accomplished. The time has come, and an invincible force draws me toward the abyss where I must be crushed.

(*She takes the lyre from the hands of Hanz.*) Hanz, do not touch it ever again. It is my heritage. They call this "madness."

ALBERTUS: *Mon dieu*! Helen has again lost her wits.

HELEN, *in a sort of ecstasy, holding the lyre*: The lyre! Here is the lyre! O Lyre, how I love you!

CARL: What is she saying? See how her appearance changes!

HANZ: Her face is pale white, and her eyes glow with a celestial happiness.

ALBERTUS: Young woman, what's happening to you? A luminous halo surrounds you!

HELEN, *speaking to the lyre*: For long I have wanted to hold you thus. You know how I have respected you as a sainted offering placed between heaven and me.

CARL: What sublime language!

ALBERTUS: You swore to your dying father never to touch this lyre, which he believed enchanted. The fantasies of the dying should be sacred, like the decrees of wisdom. My child, beware the affect of sound on your weakened brain.

CARL: Dear Helen, you are not well. I don't know what all this means, but listen to Master Albertus. He is a wise man and one who loves you.

HELEN, *speaking to the lyre*: I have not profaned you and my hands are pure. You know it well. I have such longing to know you and to unite myself with you. Don't you want to speak to me? Am I not your daughter? (*To Albertus and Carl, who want to take the lyre from her*) Leave me alone, men. I have nothing in common with you. I am no longer of your world. (*To the lyre*) I belong to you. Do you wish at last to be mine?

HANZ, *to Albertus*: O Master, leave her alone. Respect her ec-stasy. See how beautiful she is, bent to the ground on one knee. See how gracefully she rests the lyre on the other knee and how her alabaster arms embrace the lyre with love!

ALBERTUS: You don't realize to what peril the young enthusi-ast is abandoned. Fear for her reason, for her life, which have been compromised by the sound of the lyre.

HANZ: Look, Master! There is some marvel at work here. The ribbons of her hair break and fall at her feet. Her locks seem animated as though a magic breath disengages them from their shining bonds to scatter them down her brow and pour them out in a flood of gold over her snowy shoulders. Yes, see how her hair billows out in free and lusty rings, like those of a young child that runs in the morning wind. It glistens, it flares, it streams over her beautiful body, like a cascade seized with fire from the sun. O Helen, how beautiful you are now! But you don't hear me.

ALBERTUS: Hanz, my son, do not look at her too much. There are in human life some mysteries that we have not yet grasped and that I did not suspect until now. (*Aside*) Oh, I too feel trou-bled. I wish I did not see this sibyl.[22]

HELEN (*She takes up the lyre in one hand and raises the other toward the sky.*): Behold! The mystery is accomplished. Life is short, but it is full. Man has only a day, but this day is the dawn of eternity. (*The lyre resounds magnificently.*)

HANZ: O muse! O beauty inspired!

CARL: What a celestial melody! What a marvelous hymn! My ears have never heard the like, and insensible as I usually am

22. In classical literature, a prophetess, like the Sibyl of Cumae whom Aeneas meets in Book 6 of Virgil's *Aeneid*. On the sibyl as a female symbol, see the introduction.

to music, I feel my eyes flooded with tears and my spirit transported to regions unknown before.

ALBERTUS, *lowering his voice*: Keep quiet, or at least speak softly. Watch the marvel. There is much to learn here. Don't you see that her hands are not touching the strings? Her left arm alone supports the instrument, leaning on her breast. As if the beating of her burning heart, as if a divine breath coming from her sufficed to make the strings vibrate, without the aid of any human art the lyre sings some strange song in an unknown mode.

HANZ: Yes, I see the marvel. I knew well that this creature belonged to a higher world. Let me hear her, Master. She has not finished. God, into what ravishings she plunges my entire being! Yes, Master, the soul is immortal, and after this life infinity will open up before us.

(*Helen makes the lyre sing, and Albertus converses in a low voice intermittently with his two students. The words which the spirits sing are not heard by men, and only the melody of the lyre, of which the words are the expression, strikes their ears.*)

CHORUS OF SPIRITS OF HARMONY: Your moment has come, our brother Spirit, whom a magic power holds captive in the heart of this lyre. We have heard your melodious voice, and we shall fly about your ivory prison until the hand of this virgin has become strong enough to break the charm and set you free. Already you are no longer condemned to silence. A pure breath reanimates you. Hope! Man can determine nothing, and what has been ravished from the sky must return there.

SPIRIT OF THE LYRE: O my brothers! O well-beloved spirits! Approach, descend toward me! Hold out your hands! Snatch me from this prison, that I may fly with you in the pure air above the sterile regions where men live. O my brothers, do not abandon me! I gasp, I tremble, I suffer. Hear my sighs, hear my timid tears, carry me on your wings of fire.

SPIRITS OF HARMONY: The magician has bound you with seven strings of metal. For you to emerge from the lyre, a hand free of all uncleanness must break the seven strings one by one. But it must be the hand of a human creature. We can only assuage your grief by our song and animate your hope by our presence.

SPIRIT OF THE LYRE: Oh, pity me, console me, speak to me! For I am a captive and I grieve, I tremble, I suffer, I weep.

ALBERTUS: The sound of the lyre is grievous, and its song is one of a mortal sadness. O Helen, what is going on in your soul to make your inspiration so heartrending?

WILHELM: The rhythm throughout was most grand, the sound most powerful, the inspiration most triumphant. It could have been called a hymn and now one could call it a prayer.

CARL: As for me, I understand nothing of it. But I suffer, and yet I cannot pull myself away from here.

SPIRITS OF HARMONY: Brother, we will tell you of your father-land and you will be consoled. We come from the white light that men, your companions in misery, call Vega and which they have dedicated to the lyre.[23] Your native light, young brother, is as pure, as bright, as serene as the day, where a magical power has caused you to descend in order to live among men. It is always governed by the same sound. The whole ray of the infinite prism always sings of the life of this star.

---

23. Vega (Wega in Sand's text) is the bright star in the constellation known as The Lyre.

(*Neighbors, drawn by the music, penetrate*[24] *into the garden and appear at the door of Albertus's study.*)

AN ADMIRER: Behold the instrument, little used, but of an incomparable quality and range of sound. It is without doubt a work of monsieur Meinbaker.

ANOTHER ADMIRER: Probably. But aren't you amazed by the talent of his daughter? I don't believe there is a similar virtuoso in the world. And she pretended not to know music!

A MERCHANT: Gentlemen, you have been standing behind us. You don't see. Come forward a little and explain to us, since you are connoisseurs, how Mlle Meinbaker can play this instrument without touching the strings.

FIRST ADMIRER, *looking at Helen*: It is really very strange. I had not noticed.

A MERCHANT'S WIFE: This smells too much of sorcery. I want to get away from here. I had always suspected that sly old Meinbaker of being addicted to some secret art. He never went to church and he was much too involved with Master Albertus, who is himself . . .

FIRST ADMIRER: Be assured, madame, there is nothing less of sorcery than this manner of playing. This lyre is a kind of organ that is constructed like a clock and that plays without human touch, as long as the spring has not completed a certain number of turns on the pivot.

A YOUNG WOMAN: I assure you, monsieur, that Helen is playing with her eyes. See, she turns pale, she blushes, her eye shines or grows dim, and the music becomes slow or fast,

24. Feminist critics may be interested in the recurrence of the verb "penetrate" throughout the rest of the play.

sweet or harsh, by her wish. I believe that poor Helen has been bewitched by it.

SECOND ADMIRER: How's that, mademoiselle? You don't see that what you take for your friend Helen is an automaton, made to resemble her. We speak of Helen, of course, but it is quite simply a machine, and you are going to see it stop. The eyes are enamel and turn on a spring. The breathing is produced by a bellows in the body of the mannequin . . . [25]

SPIRITS: We have spoken enough to you. Now give your attention to your liberator. Reflect that she alone can break the spell. It is your task to instruct her and to reveal yourself to her if her intelligence can raise itself to your level.

SPIRIT OF THE LYRE: What, already, my brothers? What do you want me to become without you, here in my tomb of ivory? What can I say to a daughter of men?[26] She will not understand my language. Oh, I tremble, I suffer, I weep.

HELEN, *ceasing to play and rising energetically*: You spoke! You said, "I suffer, I weep." Who then are you?

YOUNG WOMAN, *to the Second Admirer*: Do you think it is an automaton now?

ALBERTUS: Helen, that is enough. The lyre has spoken well. Don't press the proof too far. The sound of this instrument is too powerful for human ears. It confuses our ideas and makes our reason wander. (*He takes the lyre from her.*)

25. Compare the variant tradition in the Helen legend, as in Stesichorus and Euripides' *Helen*, according to which the real Helen was replaced in Troy by an *eidolon* or mannequin. On automata in Sand's time, see A. W. K. G. Ord-Hume, *Clockwork Music* (London, 1973), pp. 18–62.

26. The phrase "daughter of men" recurs frequently. Compare the name given to Jesus in the gospels: "son of man." Helen becomes a sacrificial figure representing all women.

HELEN: What are you doing? Stop, let me keep it! (*She falls in a faint.*)

HANZ: O Master! Why deprive her of the lyre? You are going to kill her! Master, she seems dead, truly dead!

ALBERTUS: Don't be afraid; it's nothing. The electric current of the lyre must have produced this crisis. Carl, Wilhelm, carry her, I beg you. Room! Room! Give her air!

HELEN, *coming to* (*She repulses Wilhelm.*): Don't touch me, Wilhelm! I am not your fiancée. I will never be yours. I do not love you. You are a stranger to me. I belong to a world where you know not how to enter without dying or damning yourself.

WILHELM: O my God, what is she saying? She does not love me!

CARL: What Hanz said was right.

ALBERTUS: My child, you speak irrationally, and you will think differently tomorrow. Give me your arm that I may take you back to your room.

HELEN: No, Master Albertus, please. I will not go. I shall go to the country. I shall go to see the rising of the moon over the lake.[27]

THERESE (*Helen's governess*): You are not speaking to our master with the respect you owe him. Recover yourself, Helen. All the town hears and sees you.

HELEN: I neither hear nor see anyone. Nothing exists for me any more. I am alone forever.

27. Because the Greek word for moon, *selene*, resembles the name *Helene*, Helen was often identified with the moon, from antiquity until the nineteenth century. Both Helen and the moon are often symbols of woman; see especially act 3, scene 1.

ALBERTUS: Alas! The crisis has been too strong. She has lost her reason. Helen, Helen, obey me! I am your father. Go to your room!

HELEN: I have no father. I am the daughter of the lyre[28] and I do not know you. For a long time you made me unhappy by condemning me to some spiritual studies that are contrary to my faculties. But your big words and your long philosophical arguments are not for me. The time has come to live. I am a free being. I wish to live free. Adieu! (*She flees across the garden [i.e., out the balcony window].*)

ALBERTUS: Hanz, Wilhelm, follow her and watch over her. (*To the other students*) My friends, excuse me. This unexpected misfortune has taken from me the strength to resume the lesson. (*All exit.*)

Scene Nine

MEPHISTOPHELES, *appears and addresses the lyre*: Stubborn Spirit, who could have received from me, in an instant, liberty and life! Since you prefer to pass through seven trials and to emerge slowly from your prison, at the mercy of a human being, expect to suffer! I have enough power over all that relates to the earth to augment your griefs and prolong your agony. You scorn my help. Instead of coming with me to inhabit the regions of revolt and hate, you prefer to return to an unjust God who betrays you, for the smallest fault, to the caprice and

28. In act 2, scene 2, Albertus will recall a story told by Helen's father, Meinbaker, which says that the soul of Adelsfreit, their ancestor, was condemned by God to live enclosed in the lyre until liberated by a hand free from sin.

slavery of man. I shall put such thoughts in the heart of Helen that you will regret having rejected me!

SPIRIT OF THE LYRE: Helen does not belong to you.

MEPH.: But Albertus will belong to me!

SPIRIT: God protect him!

ACT TWO

The Strings of Gold

Scene One

A terrace at Albertus's house. Helen, stretched out on cushions, is sleeping in the open air. Albertus approaches her cautiously. [A few days have passed.]

ALBERTUS: It is the hour when she offers up her hymn to the rising sun . . . She is still resting . . . If I hide there, under the oleanders, I'll be able to see and hear her easily. . . When she believes she is alone, she draws from her lyre some very strange melodies . . .

O woman inexplicable, creature without equal, or at least without like on earth! What mysterious bond continues to unite your destiny to that of this musical instrument? Why do you hold it so tightly in your arms during sleep, like a mother fearing someone may steal her child? How beautiful you are, though unconscious of your beauty! Helen, Helen! I do not at all profane your chaste sleep by thoughts of lust. Your figure is beautiful according to what others say, but I know nothing of that. If I admire your brow and your eyes and your long hair, it is because through these external signs called physical beauty I contemplate your intellectual beauty, your immaculate soul. It is your spirit that I love, melancholy virgin. That alone I wish to know and to possess. To unite myself intimately with it, I want to penetrate the unknown language in which it expresses itself. See, she is waking up! She adjusts the lyre, leans it against her breast. Her drooping hands do not even

touch the strings . . . and yet the strings vibrate, the lyre resounds . . . The phenomenon is beyond all my research . . .
(*He hides. The lyre sounds magnificently.*)

SPIRIT OF THE LYRE: Awake, daughter of men, for your sun
rises from the earthly horizon. Bow down your spirit before
this globe of infinite light. The sun is not God, but it is divine.
It is one of the innumerable diamonds sewn in the vestment
of God. Creation is the body or the vestment of God. Like the
spirit of God, it is infinite. Creation is divine; spirit is God.

Daughter of men, I am a portion of the spirit of God. This
lyre is my body, the sound is divine, the harmony is God. God
is in you as a ray that penetrates you, but you cannot see the
source from which this ray emanates, for this light of intelligence and love floats in the infinite. Like one of the atoms
of gold that you see shine and rise in this ray from the east,
O Virgin, you must sparkle and rise toward the light—a light
that never is hidden from pure spirits called to contemplate it.

Daughter of men, purify your heart, fashion it as a jeweler
polishes the facet of a crystal gem to make the brightness of
the prism play. Make of yourself a surface so limpid that the
ray of the universe crosses through you and embraces you.
Reduce your being to dust to assimilate yourself to it and to
lavish yourself in divine flux within its burning breast, always
consuming, always fecund. (*The lyre ceases.*)

CHORUS OF CELESTIAL SPIRITS: Hark, hark, O daughter of
the lyre, to the divine accords of the lyre universal! All this
infinity that weighs upon your being and crushes it with its
own immensity, all this can be opened before you and let
you mount like a pure flame, like a subtle spirit. Let your ears
hear and your eyes see! All is harmony, both sound and color.
Seven notes and seven colors are interlaced and are in movement around you in eternal harmony. There is no mute color;

the universe is a lyre. There is no invisible sound; the universe is a prism. The rainbow is the reflection of one drop of water; the rainbow is the reflection of the infinite. It raises in the heavens seven clear voices that chant incessantly the glory and the beauty of the Eternal. Resume the hymn, O daughter of the lyre! Join your voice to that of the light. Every grain of golden dust that dances in the solar beams sings the glory and beauty of the Eternal. Every rosy drop that glitters on every wave of a stream, every rock, every bit of moss, every insect sings the glory and beauty of the Eternal.

And the light of the earth and the pale moon, the vast planets and all the lights of infinity with the innumerable worlds they illuminate, and the splendors of the shining ether and the unmeasurable empyrean depth of the sky, all hear the voice of the grain of sand that rolls down the slope of a mountain, the voice that an insect produces while unfolding its diaphanous wings, the voice of a flower that dries and bursts while letting fall its seed, the voice of the flowering moss, the voice of the leaf that expands to drink the rosy dew; and the Eternal hears all the voices of the universal lyre. It hears your voice, O daughter of men, as well as that of the constellations. For nothing is small to that before whom nothing is grand, and nothing is contemptible to the one who has created all.

Color is the manifestation of beauty; sound is the manifestation of glory. Beauty is celebrated continually on all the strings of the infinite lyre; harmony is continually given life by all the rays of the infinite light. All voices and rays of the infinite thrill and vibrate continually before the glory and beauty of the Eternal.

ALBERTUS: How is it, I wonder, that Helen seems to hear sounds inaudible to my ears? The lyre is silent, yet Helen is seized in ecstasy, as if something hovers over her, speaking to her . . . See how she takes up the lyre, as though pressed to reply! What then has she heard? (*The lyre resounds.*)

SPIRIT OF THE LYRE: O my brothers, speak again to the daughter of men! Help me teach her that she may know me, that she may love me, and that she may deliver me. Make her understand the mysteries of the infinite and the grandeur and immortality of mankind, this divine atom that the breath of God inspires, without stopping, to nourish and to populate another abyss of the infinite. (*The lyre grows silent.*)

CHORUS OF SPIRITS: O Spirit enchained, you must pass through many trials. Bound by the conjuration of the seven strings, you cannot be freed except by suffering. Such is the destiny of all who reside among humanity. This land is a land of sorrows. One descends there only for expiation, one leaves only by expiation. (*The lyre resounds.*)

SPIRIT OF THE LYRE: O Purgatory! O suspense! O terror! Shall I then lose perception of the infinite? Must I swim in doubt and ignorance, like mortal men? Must I wander in darkness, deprived of divine light? . . . Daughter of men, must I inhabit your soul, a darker and colder prison than the lyre? . . . (*Helen puts her hands on the strings of the lyre and makes them vibrate loudly.*)

ALBERTUS: What do I hear? What new harmony! Sounds strong and sweet at once. This music is less learned, more soft . . . I think I am going to understand it . . . But what do I see? . . . Helen is touching the strings; it is her soul that speaks.

SPIRIT OF HELEN, *while Helen plays the lyre* (*The words of Helen are heard only by the spirits. The sound of the lyre is the expression for human ears.*): Why do you fear me, ungrateful and rebellious spirit? You are not God as you boast; you are a son of men, you too, son of science and pride. Look at me and see if I am not as pure as the most pure crystal. See if I am not flooded with the ray of the infinite, fired by the respect for God. Do not disdain me because I dwell in the breast of a mortal virgin. This virgin is a spotless sacrifice. A celestial love can inspire her to offer herself up for you in a holocaust and to take on herself the expiation to which you are condemned. (*Helen ceases playing. The lyre replies.*)

SPIRIT OF THE LYRE: I have heard you, I have seen you, O virgin immaculate. You understand me, you speak to me, your nature is revealed to me. God has permitted it. You love me, and I too love you. For I see you, and you to me resemble the most beautiful of the stars. Oh, let a celestial hymn bring us together! United forever, melted the one in the other, our souls will go to dwell in the infinity of worlds.

HELEN, *letting the lyre fall on the cushions*: Enough! Leave me. Your embrace consumes me, I faint . . . (*She falls in a faint.*)

ALBERTUS: This is the cataleptic fit into which she daily falls, at the same hour, after having played the lyre . . . This sleep that resembles death, this prostration that so terrified me the first few times, no longer troubles me. It restores her strength and seems a natural function of her constitution. I shall call her governess and take myself in secret to an examination of the lyre.

Scene Two

In Master Albertus's study. Albertus and Hanz are together. Albertus is seated in front of his desk; the lyre is set behind him, among books and scattered papers.

ALBERTUS: Music is an algebraic combination of different notes of the scale, able to cheer the spirit indirectly by agreeably titillating the auditory nerves. The titillation then produces a reaction throughout the entire nervous system. The result is that the brain can enter into a kind of fevered exaltation, as one observes among the dilettanti.

HANZ: O Master, music is a completely different thing, believe me.

ALBERTUS: Music can express feeling, but to represent ideas, even to portray objects—that is impossible. At very least, it is not magic, as many pretend. Moreover, here are notes, keys, staves, signs to indicate the rhythm, other signs to indicate raising or lowering pitch . . . These are not cabalistic signs. They fall within the most common knowledge and are subject to invariable logic.

HANZ: They are the simple, well-known elements whose combination becomes a mystery, a magic if you will, under the inspiration of genius: the language of the infinite.

ALBERTUS: But the language of this lyre, I tell you, is an exceptional thing, unique, completely outside the science of musicians. I know nothing of it; I don't believe in it. Never mind, I accept the hypothesis, and I say that music is only a creation, what we rightly call an "accomplishment."

HANZ: The supposed magician who created this talisman, then, made use of sounds in the same way that other magicians have used Arabic words or astronomical signs? All for the same purpose, to indicate, by certain formulae, the mysterious evolutions of the science of numbers, a science that, according to them, presides over the law of the universe without the intervention of any conscious force of Providence. Master, would you believe in magic more than in music?

ALBERTUS: Alas, I have dug laboriously in the obscure and deep mine that is called *cabal*, hoping to find there some hidden verities under the rubbish of lies and aberrations. I have found nothing but the deceit and ignorance of the Dark Ages, elements fatal to humanity and which, at every moment, place limits on the progress of the spirit. Even today, aren't people trying to revive sorcery, the power of charms and the rule of charlatans, under the name of magnetism? It is the magic of modern times.

More than that, the spirit of the philosopher is stymied by a new order of facts that destroy all the order of known laws. What should he conclude in the presence of prodigies that his senses cannot refuse to recognize? In theory, he owes it to posterity to reject nothing as impossible. In fact, he owes it to himself to distrust the evidence of his sense until reason is put in agreement with experience.

HANZ: *Mon dieu!* Could it be possible that man would have vegetated until now on this unfortunate earth without daring to raise the thick veil that holds him in brutishness, while what is needed by all—the strength and confidence to tear away this blindfold and pierce the darkness—has been bestowed only on certain superior beings? What? In the midst of blind generations who have dragged themselves over the face of the globe, without any hope other than the fallacious promises of priests, without consolation except for the vague, floating dream of another life, without morality except brutal indulgence or meaningless abstinence—would saints, astrologers, magicians, prophetesses, whatever name one calls them, *enlightened* men, throughout time, have lived in communication with the pure spirits of the invisible world and not be able to bring people like themselves to knowledge of truth that is consoling and sublime?[29] Would they have seen, face to face, God or the angels or the spirits that are God's ministers, without succeeding in promulgating a faith based on certitude, on the evidence of the senses, joined to that of the spirit? Humanity, nailed to the threshold of a bitter and desolate life, would have witnessed some of the elect cross over the gates of the ideal world, and as vengeance on their good luck, would have condemned them to the gibbet, the stake, to infamy, ridicule, and martyrdom in all its forms.

ALBERTUS: If it were so, how ridiculous and contemptible would be our own philosophy! It is we who should be scourged in public and put in the pillory, like forgers and blasphemers.

HANZ: Master, at this moment do you incline toward the sorcerers or toward the philosophers?

ALBERTUS: What do you think, philosopher's apprentice? Are you waiting for me to give the answer to the great problem of your own belief? If you doubt my conviction at this moment, it is because you are not sure about your own. If I must say all, my dear Hanz, I have strongly suspected for some time that you were losing yourself in clouds of "illuminism." Are you not in fact affiliated with some secret society?[30]

---

29. As the Swedish philosopher, Emanuel Swedenborg (1688–1772), attempted to do through his new revelations of Christianity. The thought and syntax of this passage are difficult. Knowledge has not been bestowed only on "superior beings," though prophets have arisen and have tried to communicate their visions, and some have suffered for it. The answer implied to each of Hanz's questions is "no."

30. Illuminism is the belief in a special personal enlightenment. In *The Countess of Rudolstadt* (especially chapter 41), Sand has much to

HANZ: For some time, Master, you have been making fun of me in order to avoid my questions. I would be happy to see you in such good humor if I didn't know that among serious spirits irony is not an indication of calmness and interior contentment. You always teach with remarkable ability, but, if you must know, your lectures no longer seem to me as clear, nor your conclusions as cogent. Apparently a new chain of ideas, still confused and impossible to formulate, has come to interrupt the unity of your thought. You seem put out with yourself, and I'm certain of one thing: soon you will give the last lecture in the course without really completing it, because doubt overcomes you relative to your past and, perhaps, a great light rises over you to reveal your future to you.

ALBERTUS: I see. My students doubt my honesty. They ask themselves if I have come to terms with some power, and they await in mocking silence for me to reveal, little by little, my apostasy . . .

HANZ: Master, that kind of speaking means you have lost the noble serenity of your soul. We love you, we respect you, and none of us accuses you. It is only that we see a secret disturbance gnawing at you, and we are pained at it because we were accustomed to find in your teaching hope and consolation, which we no longer find there. What becomes of the passengers when the pilot has lost his course among the reefs?

ALBERTUS: My friend, we will resume this conversation. For now, leave me alone. I am quite agitated, and I would perhaps do well to suspend my class. A new world has opened to me; I still dare penetrate there only in trembling, for I cannot enter there all alone. I know that I shall draw along with me those

---

say about eighteenth-century secret societies, including the Order of the Masons.

spirits who have put their confidence in me, and I do not want to put aside lightly the sacred trust of conscience.

HANZ: That is a scruple worthy of you. I leave you, Master. May you again find peace of soul.

Scene Three

ALBERTUS, *alone*: How he delayed me! He who takes on responsibility for the beliefs and principles of another, he who dares to involve himself in teaching and directing other men, doesn't know the burden he lays on his life. He who makes a profession of wisdom is truly a fool and truly unfortunate, when he is not a vile imposter. At the moment when he believes he possesses truth, at the moment when he climbs to the lectern to proclaim it, his eyes grow dim, and darkness descends around him, confused glimmerings dance in the obscure distance, and his mouth speaks words that no longer make sense to his spirit. Everything is only pride and lying in the empty science of man. There will perhaps be pardon above only for one who knows how to doubt and be silent. (*Taking up the lyre.*)

None the less, there is no effect without a cause. This instrument is no fancy hurdy-gurdy or accordion, as I let it be thought. I have taken it apart, piece by piece; I've carefully examined all the parts.[31] The magnificent sounds this instrument produces are due only to scientific proportions or the perfect ratio of the separate parts. I make its sonorous strings vibrate, and clearly my hand does not profane them, for their vibrations do not bring disturbance to my being. But it would be impossible for me to draw from it any harmony other than

31. This seems inconsistent with Albertus's later efforts to disconnect the strings, which then immediately break.

the simple chords that a weak notion of music permits me to form. My fingers search for them and find them. My ear hears them and judges them. But my thought could never awaken a sound on these strings. Yet the thought of Helen moved them and made them distill sublime songs, without recourse to art, without the aid of touch. The effect is well proved. I must seek the cause of it. To neglect to find it would be the act of a lazy coward or stupid pride . . . Why then do I tremble in approaching this object? It is there, before me, like a river of fire from which arise eddies of smoke. It seems to me that, like astrologers of the Middle Ages, I am going to leave the pure air of the sky and the light of the sun for the darkness of hell and the illusions of Satan . . . I shall know, nevertheless, how to vanquish these silly terrors. From now on in the imagination of men there are neither Tartarus[32] nor demons; there is doubt there, nothingness still more frightful. Help me, divine hope, fruit of my long travail and of my painful austerity.

Scene Four

MEPHISTOPHELES, *aside* (*He enters in the figure of the Jew.*): In this state of mind you greatly please me. I am going to stick some pricks of curiosity into your lazy brain. (*Aloud*) I bow before Your Stoicism.

ALBERTUS: I am your servant. What do you want of me?

MEPH.: Your Infallibility does me not the honor of recollecting me.

ALBERTUS: Perhaps I saw you in a lunatic hospital?

MEPH.: Your Austerity jokes. I am the good Israelite, Jonathas Taer.

32. Tartarus is the underworld in classical mythology.

ALBERTUS: I recognize you now. But since report of your death circulated here I did not expect this meeting.

MEPH.: I have been gravely ill in Hamburg. All the doctors expected my death. But at the moment when they claimed I must be buried, I found myself on my feet, thanks to a remedy that a fortune-teller brought me. I have reason to believe that those medical gentlemen, to avoid disappointment, had a log buried in my place. My recovery would have ruined their reputations.

ALBERTUS: Why so? You both could have been right. Your malady was mortal, but Jews are tough. Tell me what you want. No useless compliments, I beg. My time is not always at my own disposal.

MEPH., *aside*: Cad! Who knows better than I the time you waste chasing will-o'-the-wisps! (*Aloud*) My dear sir, I come to propose a deal.

ALBERTUS: Oh, that was your refrain with my dear friend Meinbaker. But what business could you have with me? I have nothing and I don't want anything.

MEPH.: I have here in my pocket some papers that I am sure will interest you.

ALBERTUS: Some papers?

MEPH.: A valuable manuscript.

ALBERTUS: Let's see it. No, never mind. You don't do anything for nothing and I couldn't pay. Don't tempt me. Keep it.

MEPH.: Looking costs nothing. These are documents that came into my hands as payment at the sale after the death of Master Meinbaker. I was one of his creditors and like so many others was ruined.

ALBERTUS: When a Jew complains, it's a sign he is content. From whom came the manuscript?

MEPH.: From whom could it come but from the great lute-maker, poet, composer, instrumentalist, and magician, Tobias Adelsfreit?

ALBERTUS: Ah, I've seen much of his writing.

MEPH.: I'm much reassured. You can establish the authenticity of this. (*He spreads out some old notebooks on the desk.*)

ALBERTUS: Really, it seems to me beyond doubt. There's his signature and seal . . . contracts for the sale of various instruments . . . inventories of the shop at different times, with date of manufacture of the instruments. All this is unimportant. But this book with strange figures, half effaced by time . . . it's still his writing. Let's see, are these verses? No. Here are some attempts at musical composition, lyrics of great value doubtless for the curious, and of great interest to artists . . . What do I see here? Some disconnected words—some truncated phrases, jotted down as reminders. It would be useless or impossible to reconstruct their meaning. (*Talking to himself and oblivious of the presence of Mephistopheles*) Ah now, some cabalistic signs, some magic! I'm sure of it. Our ancestors could not escape their crude perceptions without falling into superstitions still more crude. Should I be surprised at that? Even I, who live in a century of enlightenment and coolly judge the errors of the past, even I, ten times a day, feel the temptation to believe in these absurdities. It is a consequence of the imperious need man feels to escape from the positive by one door or another, even if by the door that leads to madness.

MEPH., *aside*: You will enjoy it. This door is large, and you will pass through without bowing your head. (*Aloud*) Master, do not let your learning scorn these characters of necromancy. Our ancestors often experimented with this barbarous language of ideas, as wise and philosophic as you are able to be today. Although these concepts seem to you vague and mysterious, they always retain a certain profundity, which would give you material for thought if you could read them.

ALBERTUS: You push your merchandise with much enthusiasm, Master Jonathas. But I will tell you that it tempts me little. Adelsfreit wrote some good poetry, but I don't see any in these records. Music and magic are hardly my field, neither one nor the other.

MEPH.: What if this so-called magic were only a mysterious way to express freely ideas so advanced that the barbarism of that age did not want to admit to them? What if, by searching carefully, you were going to discover there a scroll of new insight and unexpected revelation? For example, if I translate this passage here literally . . . (*He takes one of the manuscripts and reads.*) "A time will come when men will have all the intelligence and feeling of the infinite. Words will no longer be the language of the senses but 'the other' will be that of the spirit."

ALBERTUS: What does he mean by "the other?" Music?

MEPH., *aside*: Ah, we are beginning to catch his ear! (*Aloud, and continuing to read*) "All intelligent being will be a lyre and this lyre will sing only for God. The language of rhetoricians and dialecticians will be vulgar language. Intelligent beings will hear the songs of the higher world. As the eye will seize upon the magnificent spectacle of the heavens and will comprehend the hidden marvels of infinite order, the ear will grasp the sublime concert of the stars and will comprehend infinite harmony. This will not be a victory of the senses, but a victory of the spirit. It is the spirit that will see the movement of the stars; it is the spirit that will hear the voice of the stars. The spirit will have its senses, just as the body has its. It will transport itself into the worlds of the infinite and will leap the abyss of the infinite. This task has been begun on earth. Man rises, through each century, through a hundred thousand and a hundred million wanderings, above the mud from which he came. It is a long way from the corybantes[33] whom the clash of bronze shields threw into frenzy to the Christians who prostrate themselves when hearing the blast of an organ. Man will finally understand that if metal has a voice, if wood, if the viscera and the throat of animals, if the wind, the lightning, the waves have voice; if he himself, through his bodily organs, has a powerful voice; his soul and the universe, which is the father of the soul, have voices to call out and to respond to one another. He will understand that the power of harmony is not in the sound produced by wood or metal, still less in the childish exercise of the fingers or the throat, no more than perpetual movement is in machines of wood or metal that an industrious hand can create. The senses are only servants of the spirit. What the spirit does not understand, the hand cannot create. I shall create a lyre without equal. The most solid ivory, the purest gold, the most sonorous wood will be utilized. I shall apply all the science of the musician, all the art of the instrument maker. The most skilled and practiced hands will draw from it only vulgar song, unless the spirit directs them and unless divine breath enfolds the spirit. O Lyre, spirit is in thee as it is in the universe. But you will be mute if the spirit does not speak." Well, Master, do you begin to understand?

ALBERTUS: Certainly all this gives a poetic sense of an order that is perhaps very elevated, but for me it is excessively vague.

33. Priests of the ancient Phrygian goddess, Cybele.

MEPH.: Don't be discouraged. Seek, over time, this mysterious sense. It may be that Adelsfreit did not discern it clearly himself. Even men most gifted with perception of the ideal still have only glimmerings. An idea is something toward which many generations of superior men work their way. They all complement each other. But each has formulated it, imperfectly, in his own way. You must combine together these separate elements in the distillery of your brain to draw out its quintessence.

ALBERTUS: You speak too well for a simple secondhand dealer, Master Jonathas. I suspect you of affecting this business for appearance's sake and of being at heart given to studies you do not want to be known. Say, what are you? Philosopher or necromancer?

MEPH.: Both the one and the other, sir.

ALBERTUS: As in the Middle Ages? That is seen no more. You are the last of the race.

MEPH.: I am a man of my age more than you are, Honorable Master. I am at one and the same time adept at reason and a partisan of magnetism. I am a spiritual follower of Spinoza. I reject nothing, I examine all, I choose what is easiest for me to do. I look at all things from above; I am a little of the skeptic. Moreover, I am very sympathetic to all new ideas and all ancient ones. In a word, I am eclectic, that is to say that I believe in everything because I believe nothing.

ALBERTUS: You are joking, or at least you mock yourself with much spirit.

MEPH.: You take me for somewhat mad, my good sir. Beware of being somewhat too wise yourself. I have carefully followed your lectures for some time. Although I have never tried to attract your attention, amid the crowd I am perhaps the only man alive who has understood you and who is well acquainted with you.

ALBERTUS: You, sir!

MEPH.: Without doubt. I know that you are exactly the opposite of me. You believe in nothing, because you believe everything. But come, I don't want to inconvenience you for long. Let me leave you these papers. I assume you will read them with pleasure. You understand Arabic script, and the more you examine these things, the more you will find there to your taste.

ALBERTUS: But I am unable to buy them from you . . .

MEPH.: I lend them to you. I will find an opportunity to dispose of them. For payment, I ask the favor of coming to debate with you sometime. Don't be angry. I know a little about everything, even music. If you want, we will put together a work to explain the harmonico-magnetic phenomenon that makes this lyre play by itself in the arms of Helen.

ALBERTUS: Helen! What do you know of Helen?

MEPH.: Oh, your beautiful ward is not so hidden away in your house that rumor of her miraculous madness has not spread through the town. Moreover, I have often lingered near here while she magnetized her lyre, and I recognized, from the sounds she drew from it, the nature of the instrument as well as that of her seizure.

ALBERTUS: Sir, you are now speaking of something that much interests me, and if you have some notions about this phenomenon, I beg you, in the name of science and of truth, communicate them to me.

MEPH.: So you are not averse, monsieur the philosopher! But you would have too much logic to understand what I would venture to explain to you.

ALBERTUS: Perhaps on the contrary I would not have enough. Nevertheless, I will force myself to put aside all philosophical pride.

MEPH.: No, you have too much prejudice. Reason, that is to say obstinate love of evidence, is the most opinionated of false ideas.

ALBERTUS: Alas, sir, you don't know what you are saying. And perhaps you are nearer the truth than you think in saying just now that because of believing everything I believe in nothing.

MEPH.: Ah, take care not to fall into blasphemy, my poor friend. It is still necessary to believe in something, be it one's own ignorance.

ALBERTUS: I have paid for believing in mine. For the last two months I have watched every day, before my eyes, the occurrence of the phenomenon of which we were just speaking. It is still impossible for me to formulate, in this regard, a theory that even begins to satisfy me.

MEPH., *aside*: Watch, I am going to confound all your grand ideas with some words. (*Aloud*) I can well believe it, my dear sir. You are ignoring a host of things that you misunderstand and that yet will open to you the doors to a world unknown. For example, I wager you have never heard magnetic harps play.

ALBERTUS: I have heard aeolian harps, played by the wind.

MEPH.: And you do not regard the thing as impossible?

ALBERTUS: Certainly not.

MEPH.: You admit that the air can make a harp play, and you do not admit that human breath, moved by will, by thought, by inspiration, can produce similar effects?

ALBERTUS: It would be necessary to suppose in such instruments an incredible delicacy of impression for one to make it speak.

MEPH.: Suppose still more. Suppose there exists a sympathetic rapport between the artist and the instrument.

ALBERTUS: That is exactly what I cannot admit.

MEPH.: Relax. Suppose nothing, admit nothing. But, for the sake of being logical, you must then deny the existence of a phenomenon you see accomplished every day right before your eyes.

ALBERTUS: I admit all that you prove to me.

MEPH.: Let's see. Do you sincerely want to know the secret of the magnetic lyre?

ALBERTUS: I want to.

MEPH.: And you will not bring to this study your scientific pride and your stubbornness as a logician?

ALBERTUS: I promise to listen with the simplicity of a child learning to read.

MEPH.: Very well. As it were, learn to read. Study these manuscripts and then, afterward, you shall carefully examine this instrument.

ALBERTUS, *smiling*: And that's all?

MEPH.: I'll come back to explain the rest when you have studied your lesson.

ALBERTUS: Let it be so.

MEPH., *aside*: Let's leave him alone. My presence will intimidate him and keep him from indulging the childish curiosity that devours him. His philosophic seriousness embarrasses him in my presence. Alone, by himself, he is going to torment the lyre, like a child who pulls out the feathers of a bird's wing to see what makes it fly. Spirit who opposes me, you think you will be saved by Helen! But I have just aroused a terrible enemy for you, the opinionated curiosity of a logician! (*To Albertus, who is lost in thought*) I am forced to leave you, but I'll return soon. Work while awaiting me. Be assured that there is no strange thing a persevering and conscientious spirit cannot understand.

ALBERTUS: I agree. God keep you!

MEPH.: And you as well—unless the devil is the stronger and shrewder! (*He makes himself disappear.*)

ALBERTUS, *alone*: That's a strange man. Surely a charlatan, maybe a swindler. He allures me by his stories so he can sell me dearly his manuscripts . . . It doesn't matter. Looking costs nothing, he says. (*He reads the manuscript.*) Eh, here is something destitute of sense:

"Spirit who loves me and who wishes to return to God, I know how to bind you to the lyre. The footprint of the spirit of man is as immortal as genius itself. It is the seed that must impregnate the genius of other men until, absorbed and transformed by it, its own appearance fades. But it is then that it rises toward the sky like a trail of fire after having kindled the field destined to feed the sacred fire."

Could the passage be interpreted this way: All power emanates from God and, poured into the breast of man, must accomplish a mission on the earth? The life of the man who has been invested with it does not suffice to develop it. That is why the ability is given him to give it substance here below, materializing the power in some work. This work, which survives man, is no longer man himself; it is the inspiration he has received, it is the spirit he possessed during his life. This spirit must return to God, for nothing that emanates from God strays or perishes. But before returning to its source, this bit of divinity must embrace new souls and contract a sort of celestial marriage with them. Then only is its destiny accomplished and then only the creative spirit can return to God with the spirit it engendered. From their marriage arises a new spirit that, in turn, fulfills a similar destiny among men. This is how genius is immortal on earth, just as spirit is immortal in the bosom of God. . . .

Yes, doubtless that was the thought of Adelsfreit, and I see that the Jew was right in saying that this pretended magic hides some grand verities. I'm glad I have in the past studied the cabalistic language. I'm sure I'll find much of interest in this book. (*He reads it again.*)

"Seven strings will preside over your formation, O magic lyre. Two strings of the most precious metal will sing the mystery of the infinite. The first of the two is dedicated to celebrating the ideal, the second to singing faith. The one will speak the rapture of intelligence, the other the ardor of the soul. Enlightened by this spectacle of the infinite . . . " (*He lets the book fall.*)

It seems to me this takes us into pure necromancy . . . Yet if one goes back to the origin of the lyre, emblem of poetry among the ancients, one sees each string added to the instrument to mark a progress in genius and in the moral grandeur of man. Among the Chinese, the gods themselves are charged with revealing to the first lawgivers the important mystery of a new string added to the lyre, emblem of civilization among that hardworking, positive people . . . [34] Where will the history of music lead? Who will explicate to us the fabulous power that poetic history attributes to it among the elements, among barbarous peoples, among wild animals? . . . Could a simple effect of sensation have produced such powerful results, natural as one may suppose them, if it is stripped of allegory? How does it happen then that I don't comprehend this musical language? For two weeks I've zealously studied the rules of music, and it's done nothing to clarify the mystery I pursue. I've found in music a kind of arithmetic, nothing more . . . All right, the lyre of Adelsfreit has in fact strings of different metals. Here are two of pure gold. Infinity? Faith? Intelligence and Love? Those are the words Hanz and Wilhelm used to describe the sense of the hymn that rises every morning when Helen makes the lyre resound. Very well. There is one way to make sure. That is to disconnect these two strings and, if the harmony the lyre produces then changes its nature, if we perceive a different effect, I shall begin to believe that there exists a certain relationship between sounds and ideas. (*He tries to disconnect the two gold strings of the lyre.*)

What difference does it make to Helen whether the lyre has seven strings or only five? Her fingers rarely touch it. O Adelsfreit, is Helen the soul that your spirit, materialized in the work of the lyre, must impregnate?[35] Helen is a pure and beautiful improviser, but hers is hardly a superior intelli-

34. Some information on the Chinese lyre (or lute), *ku-chi'in*, had come to France from the account by Fr. Amiot in *Mémoires concernant l'histoire, les sciences, les arts, etc. des Chinois*, vol. 5 (Paris, 1780), pp. 54–58.

35. This might be open to the charge of incest, but presumably Sand did not think that the concept was applicable to the spirit world.

gence. She is ignorant of all that the science of man has accomplished. Her soul is dulled in a sort of soft and permanent alienation. Her lyrical improvisation is a phenomenon until now unobserved in this cataleptic state people today call magnetic—a new word, obscure and undefined, like the state it denotes. But still, can Helen, in the inaction where her faculties sleep, be raised toward the summit of metaphysics, while I, who have worked thirty years to enlarge my intelligence, cannot penetrate the mystery of the unknown algebra?

Damned string, it's broken! What a horrible cry came from the lyre! My blood is frozen in my veins. Ah, my poor spirit is tired, and I'm not far from having hallucinations. My brain is more exhausted in an hour abandoned to these chimeras than in a year following the thread of logic. Why then try to fight in a void? Human language is a divine attribute that distinguishes man from beast and that serves to determine, to define, to classify the most abstract ideas, to render the most complex propositions clear as the light of day. Could it also be a vulgar language and could the cadence of the nightingale be the language of the infinite? Cursed paradoxes of artists and poets, you only serve to mislead the judgment! (*The second string of gold breaks in Albertus's hands.*)

Again! This bitter cry tears my soul. What power the nervous emotions can exercise on the brain! Fatal and dangerous power, the wise man should hold himself on guard against you . . . these arts should be proscribed from the ideal state . . . No. Sounds are not ideas. At most, music can express sensations—and even that will be in a very vague and very imperfect way.

THERESE, *running in*: Master Albertus! Helen has awakened. She is anxiously looking for the lyre.

ALBERTUS: I am going to bring it to her. (*Aside*) It's the poor creature's only joy. I'll return the lyre to her and shall listen to it no more. (*To Wilhelm, Hanz, and Carl, who advance from the other side*) My boys, logic governs the universe, and he who cannot be led by it cannot pass among us to the state of certainty. Prepare everything for the lesson. I shall be with you in a moment. (*He leaves.*)

HANZ: It seems to me that his good genius has taken control over him.

CARL: It's possible, but his appearance is very altered. Believe me, he is in love with Helen. You can't be a lover and a philosopher at the same time.

WILHELM: Let's not speak lightly of this man. He suffers, but his soul can only grow through trials. (*They exit.*)

MEPHISTOPHELES [*materializing*]: Very good! I will bring such trials upon him that his soul will not resist. Since Helen no longer belongs to me, since spirit triumphs, my hate will fall entirely on the philosopher, and his soul is the lyre that I shall know how to break!

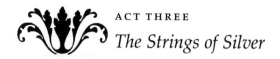

ACT THREE

The Strings of Silver

Scene One

Beside some water [in the woods.] Albertus, Carl, Wilhelm, and Helen, the latter seated on the edge of a brook, a little apart from the rest.

ALBERTUS: The sun has gone down; the coolness begins to make itself felt. The time has come for Helen to return home. It is not a good idea to prolong her first promenade too long.

WILHELM: A little while longer, my dear Master. The evening is so beautiful! The sky is still aglow with the fire of the setting sun. Helen seems to be enjoying a sense of well-being that I would hate to disturb.

CARL: Certainly for the last two months I have not seen her in such good health as tonight. Her appearance is calm, her eyes gently rapt. She still does not answer our questions, but she hears them and understands. I am sure she will recover and that soon she will be able to recount to us the beautiful visions she has had. Hanz, you believe it too, don't you? You have noticed how, every day, she has been less distraught than usual. One could say she makes a great internal effort to re-capture real life.

ALBERTUS: I tried yesterday to calm her spirit by raising it to-ward thought of God. She listened attentively, and her looks, her short replies, proved to me that I had been understood.

But when I had finished speaking she said to me "I know all that. You could have expressed it in one word."

HANZ: And what was that word? Did she tell you?

ALBERTUS: Love.

WILHELM: O Master, Helen is not mad. She is inspired!

ALBERTUS: Yes, she is a poet. It is a sort of madness, a sublime madness. One would like a moment to learn and rightly understand where inspiration ends and where illness begins.

HANZ: Good Master, haven't our long discussions on the subject at all modified your ideas? For you had promised me to reflect on it seriously.

ALBERTUS: I have reflected, but after all one must understand music. I observe Helen; I hear the lyre. I try to take account of the impressions I receive. They seem to me so different from yours that I don't dare to decide. I am trying to perceive the meaning of these learned melodies. But I swear that I have learned nothing until now that adequately enlightens me.

HANZ: What, Master, have you felt nothing more?

ALBERTUS: I felt a strange emotion, but I was no more able to analyze and define it than the music that caused it.

HANZ: Doesn't it seem to you that this music expresses ideas, rather more images than sentiments?

ALBERTUS: More sentiments than ideas, more images than sentiments.

HANZ: But what images?

ALBERTUS: Vague images of a splendor that is infinite, unapprehensible.

CARL: What's the matter, dear Helen? What are you anxiously seeking?

WILHELM: Don't expect her to reply; she doesn't even hear you.

ALBERTUS: Perhaps she hears me today. Helen, what do you desire?

HELEN: Who speaks to me? You!

ALBERTUS: I, your brother.

HELEN: My brother is not of this world.

ALBERTUS: Your father.

HELEN: Nor is my father.

ALBERTUS: Your friend.

HELEN: Ah, my friend the philosopher. Listen now! You are a learned man; you know the secrets of nature. Speak to this brook.

ALBERTUS: What shall I say to it?

HELEN: Tell it to be silent that I may hear the music from on high . . .

ALBERTUS: What music?

HELEN: I can't tell you. But you can't tell the brook to stop. This cascade sings too loudly.

ALBERTUS: It would be in vain for me to order the wave to suspend its course. God alone can command the elements.

HELEN: Don't you know a single word of the language of God?

ALBERTUS: Strange girl! Is her delirium full of an unknown poetry?

HANZ: The lyre is hung in the branches of this willow. Do you want me to give it to you, Helen?

HELEN: Hurry! The brook mocks the philosopher. It raises its voice higher and higher. (*Hanz gives her the lyre.*)

ALBERTUS, *aside*: She does not notice the absence of the two strings.

HELEN: Listen, brook, and submit! (*She touches the lyre. At the first note the brook stops running.*)

ALBERTUS: What is this new marvel? Do you see? The stream remains immobile and suspended on the rock, like a fringe of crystal!

HELEN: Flow, beautiful brook, but sing in whispers.

WILHELM: The brook resumes its flow, carefully, as if it feared to waken the flowers sleeping on its banks. (*Helen plays the lyre.*)

SPIRIT OF THE LYRE: Now the assembled earth respectfully awaits the voice of the moon that comes to look upon its darkened face.[36] Listen carefully, daughter of the lyre. Learn the secrets of the planets. From the depth of the horizon, across the black verdure, there comes a feeble voice, but one of unbelievable purity, that mounts gently in the sonorous air. It mounts, it grows, the silver disk rises from the shroud of the earth. The earth vibrates. Space is filled with harmony. Leaves quiver on the tops of trees. The white gleam penetrates into all the openings of the wood, into thousands and thousands

36. See act 1, n. 27.

of clearings of foliage. Harken to the scales of harmonious sighs that fly above the silvered moss; to the flow of melodious tears that fall in the cups of half-opened flowers! Silence, birds of the wood! Silence, insects in the long grass! Fold your metallic wings! Silence, chattering brook! Strike not with your fall the pebbles of your bed! Silence, shivering roses; unfold without noise your heavy petals, lotus of the bank! Petulant waterfowl, ruffle not the mirror where the moon is wont to gaze upon herself! Harken to what the moon sings to you and reply to her when she has penetrated and filled you with her voice and light. Become silently intoxicated with her melancholy plaint; drink long drafts of her moist reflection! Bow down with fear, with love under the flight of white angels that swim in the slanting rays! Remark, for the sake of raising yourselves, how they have plucked you with the tips of their scented wings and how they have subtly entrusted to every bird, every insect, every stream, every branch, every flower, every blade of grass the theme of the great symphony that tonight the earth must sing to the stars.

HANZ: Master, does not this music speak to your soul?

ALBERTUS: It would not know how to speak to my reason. It rouses in me some unknown instinct of contemplation, but how, I do not know. I could not translate what I hear or what I feel. Yet I give it all my attention.

WILHELM: Listen now! The rhythm changes.

SPIRIT OF THE LYRE: Now the moon is risen. She reigns on high, she shines, she bathes herself in the ether, like a perfect pearl on the bosom of an immense ocean. The pale colors of the lunar prism dance in a circle around her. The cold seas, the vast lakes, the alabaster mountains, the snowy peaks reveal themselves and are outlined along their icy slopes. Limpid mirror, incomprehensible creation of infinite thought, peaceful torch bound to the flank of the earth, your sovereign, why do you send out into the depth of the sky this eternal cry? Why do you pour on the inhabitants of the earth an influence at once so gentle and so sad? Are you a finite world or a creation incomplete? Do you weep over an extinguished race, or are you a prey to the grief of childbirth? Are you the rejected widow or the chaste fiancée of the sun? Is your languor exhaustion from a consummated act or presentiment of fatal conception? Do you demand back your children, laid on your bosom in the dust of the tomb? Do you prophesy the misfortunes of those you carry in your womb? O moon, moon, so sad and beautiful! Are you virgin? mother? abode of death? cradle of life? Does your song, so pure, evoke the ghosts of those who are no more, or of those who are not yet born? What ghastly shades flutter over your ethereal heights? Are they in repose or on alert? Are they celestial spirits that circle round your triumphant head? Are they terrestrial spirits that ferment in your bowels and are vomited from your volcanic cold?

(*The sound of the lyre is the sole manifestation of the thought of Helen for human ears. The thoughts she expresses here are clearly understood only by celestial spirits.*)

HELEN: Why ask the star when you know all the secrets of the infinite? Even if magic ties you to my side, can you not, by memory, transport yourself in thought to the regions you once inhabited?

SPIRIT OF THE LYRE: My memory is dulled, O daughter of men! Since I began to love you, I have lost the memory of all that is beyond the confines of the earth. Interrogate the universe with me, for I can teach you only what exists here below. Do you not feel, yourself, a delicious languor seize hold of your being? Do you not feel it is sweet to be in ignorance and that without ignorance love would be nothing in the world? Let us love, let us renounce knowledge! God is with us, for he is everywhere, but his face is veiled toward us, and we are henceforth, one to another, the image of God.

HELEN: I would hope you could reveal all things to me. You promised me that, and already we have taken together our flight toward the starry spheres. Why do you now refuse to initiate me? Don't you know how to lead me to this star that shines on high, a hundred thousand immensities above the moon? That is where I would go. But you do not even want to take me to the closest of the planets!

SPIRIT OF THE LYRE: I cannot do it. I am bound by the strings of the lyre and by the love I feel for you. Daughter of men, reproach me not for the shackle with which you have laden me. I am no longer a celestial spirit. I no longer know if there exists another sky than that we perceive from this bank across the tops of the trees. Your breast is my universe. United with you, I comprehend and taste the beauties of the world you dwell in. You see how serene is the night, how harmonious the voices of this world, how they are married with the concert of the stars, and how, without knowing the mysterious meaning of the hymn they sing, they join themselves in a sublime accord to the voice of the infinite.

HELEN: How can you speak of the infinite? You don't know the language of the infinite. You sing no better now than an insect hidden in the grass or a reed bent by the waves.

SPIRIT OF THE LYRE: Helen, Helen! You promised to love me and you wanted to sacrifice yourself to save me. But you are truly a daughter of men! To the extent that spirit is subdued and gives itself to you, you want to penetrate further into the mysteries of spirit and you torture him by the constraints of an implacable curiosity. O my brother spirits, come to me! Come to the daughter of the lyre! Instruct her, or grant me memory. Show God to her, or grant me the prism that helped me to contemplate Him. Come to my aid! The funeral hymn of the moon has dimmed my flame. The strings of the lyre are out of tune from the dampness of the night. The suns of infinity shine on high with their eternal splendor, and yet I hardly see them through the veils by which the earth is covered.

CELESTIAL SPIRITS: Be resigned, brother Spirit! Your destiny must be accomplished. A fatal hand has begun to break your bonds, but you yourself must be broken on the earth before returning to the skies, and your deliverance must take place through grief, terror, ignorance, forgetfulness, weakness. Such is the eternal law. The earth draws all to it, like a magnet, and those born of it cannot leave without despair. The earth is the temple of their expiation.

SPIRIT OF THE LYRE: Ah well, I love you, daughter of love and of grief. From your breast I sense a burning attraction exhaled. I would like, fading away, to be extinguished in an immense kiss and to fall asleep on your soft breast without knowing in what world I would wake.

HELEN: Yes, the night is beautiful and the earth is enchanted. The moonbeams caress it gently, and its song is deliciously married to the song of the stars. Sing again, O beautiful creation of love and grief! Sing with your thousand voices! Awake, creatures parched by thirst for the infinite! Terrestrial spirits, beautiful sphinxes with wings of purple and azure, open your bright eyes and plunge in the breast of intoxicated flowers! Come, lazy thorn apples, sing the hymn to the stars! Already the moth that loves you dances in circles round your sleeping corolla. And you, periwinkle, raise your drooping head and do not wait until the breeze rudely shakes you to sing along! Commence your poem, O inspired nightingale, let not the hoots of the owl surpass you! Come, brook, dart among the rocks and let your flowery banks repeat your call with all the notes of joy, of desire, of love, and of distress! O my soul, what you suffer! How far away are the stars! How feeble their voice! O earth, I love you. When shall I die, O my God? O my God, where are you? When will you break the lyre? Spirit, Spirit of the Lyre, when shall I see you? When shall we be delivered?

SPIRIT OF THE LYRE: Daughter of men, you do not love me. You dream only of God. You aspire only to the infinite. You see the earth as beautiful, and how sweet it is to live on its bosom, unaware of the future, in contemplation of the present, in the pleasure of idleness, in the ears of love. Love, love what belongs to you! God perhaps will never belong to you.

HANZ: Helen's hands seek the strings again. Notice, Master, how much better she plays today and how she seems to engage in dialogue with this invisible power that makes the lyre sing.

ALBERTUS: Today it seems to me that I am on the track of a natural explanation of the marvel. This lyre could be a kind of echo. Its ingenious construction makes it suited to reproduce sounds already produced by the hand that moves the strings.

WILHELM: Master, don't you hear? The sounds produced by the hand of Helen and those produced by the strings themselves have nothing in common. They are completely different melodies. But as they do not change in tone or rhythm, you do not appreciate the continual difference of the phrases.

ALBERTUS: Clearly I am a barbarian.

HELEN, *playing the lyre*: "Perhaps never!" What frightening words! Is it possible someone could pronounce them without dying? Ah, if a man could, with certainty, say "never," soon he would cease to be. "Perhaps!" That is then the melancholy theme you incessantly repeat. During the most beautiful days of sunlight, as in the most gentle starry nights, your song is a continual aspiration toward some unknown goal. God has made very short the existence of beings you engender. For desire is imperious. And if the life of a man should be prolonged beyond one day, despair would seize his soul and consume his power of immortality. O moon, at your appearance the face of the earth is covered with tears and its breast exhales only cries, for your deathly specter and your mysterious destiny seem to fill the vault of heaven with a cry of suffering and of fear. "Perhaps never!"

HANZ, *to Albertus*: Master, you are becoming depressed. Does this song at last affect you?

ALBERTUS: It makes me ill; I don't know why.

WILHELM: As for me, it tortures me.

SPIRIT OF THE LYRE: Helen, Helen, return to yourself! Dismiss useless fears. Nature is beautiful, Providence is good! Why always aspire to an inaccessible world? What does tomorrow matter if today can give happiness? If you want to enter into immaterial life, learn the first faculty you must acquire: resignation.

The pride of man never wants to bend itself to that holy ignorance where live so many cowardly beings that populate the universe. See, daughter of the lyre, how beautiful are the flowers! Hear how the song of birds is melodious! Breathe all these sweet emanations, take in all the pure harmonies of the earth! Whoever is the author and master of these things, a thought of love presided at their creation, since it has imparted to them beauty and harmony. There is happiness enough in contemplating them. Man is ungrateful when he closes his senses to so many chaste delights.

Ah, instead of continual search to pierce the veil that separates you from the ideal, why not enjoy reality? Come with me, my sister, come! My wings will enfold you and carry you to the peaks of the mountains. We shall skim in rapid flight over the carpet of variegated flowers that the breeze makes undulate across the fields. We shall leap the torrents, sporting in the foaming prism of waterfalls. We shall steep our silvery robes in the tops of the clouds over a lake, and we shall run along all the sandy beaches, without leaving there the imprint of our feet. We shall hang from the branches of willows, and I shall seed your blond tresses with blue insects, living sapphires that drop in tears on the boughs. I shall bring you a flowery crown of iris and lotus. We shall go to search for them among slippery rocks that the feet of men have never touched, in the midst of swirling whirlpools from which ships keep their distance in fear. And we shall cross the yellow wheatfields and walk on their blond heads without their being bent. We shall climb hills quicker than deer or chamois. We shall leap the great heaths where quail and grouse hide their nests in inaccessible retreats. We shall hover, like great eagles, over marble peaks where bow or sling cannot reach. We shall pass beyond, to sit on pinnacles of ice where even a swallow does not dare to set her delicate feet, and from there, we shall see the stars shine in a purer atmosphere and take in, in a glance, the immensity of the celestial constellations. And then, casting our eyes on this earth, so beautiful, whence rise ceaselessly such touching harmonies, and projecting them across the firmament, you will feel your soul soften and your tears flow. For you will comprehend that, though God has put limits on man's knowledge, he has given in recompense to man's thought a sense of the beautiful, and to this sense he has given the inexhaustible nurture of a creation sublime to contemplate.

HELEN: Yes, contemplation is the greatest joy of mankind, and I salute you and admire you and love you, O earth, as a magnificent work of Providence. Love me too, O fertile mother. Love all your children. Pardon the indifference that wastes them and the impatience to leave that devours them. Your children are sad, O patient mother. You heap up your gifts, and they abuse them. You create a thousand delights, and they scorn them. You engender them and nurture them in your bosom, but their only cry is this: "O mother without pity, you have given me life and I asked for rest. Now, scarcely have I played the game of life and you are opening your greedy bosom to swallow me in frightful sleep. O cruel mother, since you made me live, why do you want to make me die?"

SPIRIT OF THE LYRE: Listen! Nothing dies. All is transformed and renewed. And even when your thought does not mount toward these sublime heights from which you believe it came, you will still have delicious dreams this side of the tomb. Even when your essence, chained forever to that of the earth, dissolves into its elements, still there will be a destiny for you. What would you dare to scorn in nature, O daughter of the lyre? If you understand the beauty of all the beings that crowd it, what transformation can terrify or displease you? Have you never envied the silken wings of a hesperian butterfly or the plumage of a swan? What is more beautiful than a rose? What more pure than a lily? Isn't that only the life of a flower? Is not the life of a human being also sweet, also resigned, also touching? Is a single grace forgotten or lost in this immense picture? Is a single note isolated or drowned out in this vast concert? Has not Providence a caress for the least blade of grass that flourished, as well as for the greatest man that thinks? Listen, listen! You have deceived yourself. The theme you thought you heard is not a song of doubt and agony . . . Listen more carefully, the sky says "Hope." And the earth replies "Trust." (*Helen lays down the lyre and kneels.*)

HANZ: What's the matter, dear sister? Why do your tears drop so upon your beautiful, folded hands?

WILHELM: Let her pray to God. She does not hear you.

ALBERTUS, *to Helen, who rises*: Are you, better, my child?

HELEN: I feel well.

ALBERTUS, *to his students*: It is time for her to return home. The night is becoming cold. Take her, my friends, and urge her governess to put her to bed right away.

WILHELM: Aren't you coming with us, Master?

ALBERTUS: No, I need to walk further. I shall join you soon.

CARL: Don't forget the lyre.

ALBERTUS: Leave it to me. I shall take care of it. Take care of your sister.

WILHELM: Helen, lean on my arm.

HELEN, *taking Wilhelm's arm*: Life is only a day.

CARL: Helen, let me put my coat around you.

HELEN, *putting the coat over her shoulders*: And this day sums up eternity.

HANZ: Helen, could you tell us what you were thinking of just now when playing the lyre?

HELEN: I know, but I cannot explain it to you.

CARL: But could you give a name to this improvisation that might reveal its meaning to us?

HELEN: Call it, if you wish, "The Submissive Hearts."

ALBERTUS: What about yesterday's song?

HELEN, *startled*: Yesterday, yesterday? It was "The Happy Hearts." But I cannot recover it today. I no longer remember it.

Scene Two

ALBERTUS, *alone*: There is no longer any doubt that this lyre is enchanted. It governs the elements; it governs also human thought. My soul is stricken with sadness, and without understanding the mysterious meaning of its song, I have just experienced grievous, powerful emotion. Enchanted! Is it really my mouth that pronounces and my spirit that accepts such a word? It seems to me that my existence is being destroyed. Yes, my intellectual force is in decline. Instead of fighting by reason against possibly fallacious evidence, I accept it without testing, like a *fait accompli*. Perhaps the man at that mill I see there among the poplars could quite naturally explain the strangeness of the waters suspended in their course. There must only be a chance coincidence between the moment when Helen, in her seizure, ordered the brook to stop and that when the boy at the mill closed the gate of the sluice. Not long ago I wouldn't have hesitated a single instant to criticize the crude explication of this fact by a supernatural phenomenon. Today, I am filled with doubt and I fear to analyze the mystery. Could it be that the mobile and frivolous spirit of man, forced to contemplate the august face of the truth, grows weary? Ah, doubtless when such a moment comes to a meditative spirit it must be alarmed, for this moment marks its decadence and exhaustion.

Scene Three

MEPHISTOPHELES, *emerging from the willows*: If the miller had closed the gate of the sluice just at the moment when Helen was pronouncing sacramental words, the accidental co-incidence would be a marvel much more striking than the natural event you witnessed.

ALBERTUS: That Jew again! He follows me like a shadow. By day and by night he is on my trail . . . Master Jonathas, you take much interest, it seems, in the perplexities of my spirit.

MEPH.: Master Albertus, I am interested in everything and nothing surprises me.

ALBERTUS: You are more advanced than I.

MEPH.: Much more advanced, without any doubt, for you have not even begun. Have you never heard scholars debate the relationship between sound and the movement of certain bodies? Have you not attended lectures by a scholar who recently placed before us a vase filled with water inclined over a vessel? By computing the quantity of flowing water with the force of sound of a violin, he modified the direction, the agitation, and the rapidity of flow by the bow drawn over the strings. The theory of this sympathetic action will perhaps be long discussed, but the fact is confirmed. Perhaps you may find a satisfying explanation of it in the manuscripts I left with you this morning.

ALBERTUS: It was a dark day I cast my eyes on that cursed book of spells. The extravagances with which it is filled have troubled my brain all day.

MEPH.: Yet, my Master, you performed an experiment that succeeded not badly. By unfastening two strings of the lyre, you so changed the nature of Helen's inspirations that for the first time in your life you were on the point of understanding music.

ALBERTUS, *aside*: His railleries irritate me, yet this man seems to read my mind. Evidently he knows much that I do not. Why should I not open my soul to him? His skepticism cannot affect me, and his science can draw me from the maze where I wander. (*Aloud*) Master Jonathas, were you there when Helen was playing the lyre? Did you understand its song?

MEPH.: Very well. It sang the terrestrial creation, nature, as they called it in the eighteenth century, in philosophical language. The first string of silver is dedicated to contemplation of nature, the second to Providence . . . Oh, yes, I know Adelsfreit's manuscript by heart . . . Today[37] you removed the strings of gold, that represent the infinite and faith. The poor inspired girl was quite necessarily thrown back onto hope and contemplation.

ALBERTUS: Onto doubt and melancholy. That's what I understood in her song and that's the sad impression that remains with me.

MEPH.: You must not let that distress you. If you disconnect the two silver strings you will see something quite different.

ALBERTUS: And if I disconnect the two strings of steel?

MEPH.: The lyre will sing still differently, and you will begin to read in music and poetry as you read in Bayle's *Dictionary*.[38]

---

37. The time is inconsistent with the end of act 3, scene 1, where we are told that Helen's song on that occasion was separated by a day from her song in act 2, scene 1; Albertus's removal of the golden strings followed immediately after the first song.

38. *Dictionnaire historique et critique*, by Pierre Bayle, first published in 1696 and often reprinted.

ALBERTUS: You believe that?

MEPH.: I'm sure of it. Consult the manuscript when you get home.

ALBERTUS: All right, I'll try that again. But I'll attempt not to break the strings as I involuntarily broke the first two.

MEPH.: Right. The lyre is enchanted and that can bring misfortune. Don't you feel feverish since then?

ALBERTUS: What pleasure can you get from scoffing at a sincere spirit that abandons itself to you?

MEPH.: I scoff not. Did you never hear from Master Meinbaker, father of Helen and descendant in a direct line from the famous Adelsfreit, the story of how that magician, on the day of his death, having put a last hand to the lyre, was seized with such love for his masterpiece that he asked of the Lord on high, the pope of the stars . . .

ALBERTUS: What nonsense are you telling? Meinbaker had his head full of fairy stories. He claimed that Adelsfreit asked God to put his soul into this lyre and that God, to punish him for having played with his celestial heritage, condemned him to live enclosed in this instrument until a hand, untainted with any sin, should deliver him.

MEPH.: And at the instant when he pronounced this rash vow, he suddenly died.

ALBERTUS: His spirit had been wandering for some time. It gave itself voluntarily to death.

MEPH.: All this confirms a charming allegory.

ALBERTUS: What?

MEPH.: That the scholar, like the artist, owes himself to posterity. On the day when the love of art and of science becomes an egotistical satisfaction, a man who sacrifices the advantage of other men to his own pleasure is punished in his own work. It remains buried, forgotten, useless, through the centuries. His glory is lost in the clouds with which superstition surrounds it. And for having disdained to reveal himself to his contemporaries, he is condemned to be drawn from the dust only by a spirit that profits by his discoveries and usurps his fame.

ALBERTUS: I like this interpretation. I knew well you were a more serious man than you like to seem.

MEPH.: Since you do me such honor, Master Albertus, profit from some very serious advice. Do not neglect to penetrate the mystery that seems to you still to envelop the qualities of this magnetic lyre. Be assured there are, between it and the madness of your ward Helen, a relation that it is your duty to clear up and make known. Otherwise, the stupid public will make use of a natural phenomenon to accredit its own superstitions. People will say that some diabolical things have taken place in your home, and your silence will give sanction to absurd stories they are already spreading. Magic has gone out of style, but the common people have not lost their taste for it, and some distinguished spirits like to revive their old beliefs under other names, thinking to be doing something new and escape the philosophical routine.

ALBERTUS: Right you are. My best students are the first to accept all these extravagances. I shall follow up on the experiment. To start with . . . I am going to remove the two strings of silver, but with care, in order to see, by putting them back later, if Helen resumes the song of this evening.

MEPH.: Turn the pegs very gently. (*Albertus touches the first string of silver, which breaks as soon as he puts his hand on it.*)

ALBERTUS: Heavens, already broken! It seems as though my intention is enough, without aid from my hand.

MEPH.: I warned you. This instrument is of extreme delicacy. Sympathy governs it.

ALBERTUS: How dark the sky has suddenly become. See, Master Jonathas, how the moon is hidden behind the clouds and a storm gathers over our heads.

MEPH., *laughing*: It is surely the result of this broken string! I do not advise you to touch the other one.

ALBERTUS: You take me for a child. . . . I shall turn this peg so slowly. . . . (*He touches it and the string breaks.*)

MEPH.: You turned it in the wrong direction! You are decidedly adroit, in the manner of a philosopher!

ALBERTUS: What a grievous cry issued from the bosom of the deep! Did you not hear it, Master Jonathas?

MEPH.: The grating sound of this broken string irritates the nerves of the curlews sleeping in the reeds.

ALBERTUS: What a blast of wind! The poplar trees bend like rushes.

MEPH.: There's going to be a storm. Good night, Master Albertus.

ALBERTUS: You are leaving me! Will you not explain what I am experiencing at this moment? An irresistible terror is taking hold of me. Sweat runs down my brow. Don't laugh at my distress! I agree to suffer, even to be humiliated, provided my mind is clarified and that I take, at my own cost, a step toward knowledge of the truth.

MEPH., *breaking into laughter*: The truth is you are a great philosopher and that you are afraid of the devil. (*He reveals himself in his true form. Albertus gives a scream and falls in a faint.*)

MEPH.: Now, deprived of all strings that sing of the glory or the goodness of his master, this spirit ought to be in my power. Let me try to break the lyre. Helen will die, and Albertus will go mad. (*He starts to smash the lyre.*)

CHORUS OF CELESTIAL SPIRITS: Cease, cursed one! You have no power over it. God protects what you persecute. By making the just suffer, you bring them nearer to perfection. (*Mephistopheles flies off and disappears in the mist of the stream.*)

Scene Four

ALBERTUS, *little by little recovering consciousness*: What a frightful vision! Didn't you see it, Master Jonathas? It was a hideous specter. All the pains of perversity seemed to have hollowed out his deathly cheeks. A bitter laugh, triumph of implacable hate, half opened his icy lips. And in his look I saw all the fury of injustice, all the guile of wickedness, all the unpitying rage of despair without resource. Who is that unfortunate being whose aspect withers and whose look tortures? Speak, Jonathas, do you know him? . . . But where now is the old Jew? I am alone, alone in the darkness! The hair is still standing up on my head! Ah, what feebleness has now seized me? What grief has fallen on my breast and crushed it, as a hammer shatters glass? (*He sees the lyre at his feet.*)

Ah, I remember! I once brought my impious hand to this sacred relic, dwelling of a dying soul, heritage of a pious daughter. I wanted to destroy this masterpiece of an artist, this instrument, source of the only joys sad Helen experiences. There was in this lyre a mystery I ought to have respected, but my pride, jealous of not understanding its language, and the perfidious advice of the sophistic Jew overcame me. Poor Helen! What will remain for you if you cannot sing either the force or the kindness of the All-Powerful? My crime brings with it its own punishment. The very strings that I have broken on the lyre are broken in the depth of my soul. Since yesterday, the idea of the infinite has flown from me. Bitter doubt has saddened all my thoughts, and an instant ago my confidence in God disappeared like my faith. It seemed that as long as Helen was improvising and looking at the moon, I would soon be able to comprehend the secrets of her strange poetry. Nature grew more beautiful in my eyes, and at the same time that a profound melancholy came over me, I experienced an unknown charm in savoring the languors of a contemplation both chaste and voluptuous, to which I had never dared give myself. Yes, I was beginning to learn what is religious in doubt and what is divine in dreaming . . . And now, this poetic world has slipped away. A harsh voice has thrown a cry of malediction on the stricken earth. The moon no more sheds her soft clarity across the greensward, and the insects hidden under the grass do not send forth their mysterious little chirps in the solemn silence of the night. An owl screeches and flies off toward the cemetery. The brook draws out long sighs, as if its water nymph was tearing her delicate limbs on flinty stones; the wind angrily batters the leaves and strews the flowers on the ground; reptiles hiss and brambles prick under my feet. All weeps and none sings any more, and it seems to me that it is I who have troubled the peace of this serene night by evoking despair through some unknown, wicked deed! . . .

O my God, why have I sacrificed the sweetest impressions

of my life to a vain knowledge? Why this sharp resistance when a new destiny could have opened before me? Because I did not yield to the impulse that was sweeping me toward youth, beauty, love? Helen would have loved me, perhaps, if, instead of leading her spirit off into the intricacies of reasoning, I had let her raise herself up freely toward the fantastic regions where her flight led her! Perhaps there is as much logic in her poetry as there is in my science. She would have revealed to me a new face of dignity. She would have shown me the ideal under a brighter day . . . Until now, God was communicated to me only through travail, privation, grief; I might have possessed Him in the ecstasy of joy . . . So they say, at least. They all say so. They claim to be happy, all these poets, and their tears are still ones of happiness, for they are filled with intoxication. Our serenity supplies them the image of death, and our existence in their eyes is no existence at all . . . Who then persuaded me that I was pleasing to the Lord if I followed only one path? Don't I have, myself, some abilities at poetry? Why have I suppressed them in my breast as dangerous aspirations? I too could have been a man! . . . I too could have loved.

Scene Five

HANZ [*entering in search of Albertus*]: We are worried about you, my dear Master. The rain is beginning and the storm about to break. Please take my arm, for the darkness is profound and the path is steep.

ALBERTUS: Hanz, tell me, my son, are you happy?

HANZ: Sometimes, and never really unhappy.

ALBERTUS: And your happiness, does it come . . . from wisdom? from study?

HANZ: In part, but it comes to me also from poetry and still more from love.

ALBERTUS: Are you loved?

HANZ: No, Master, Helen does not love me, but I love her, and that makes me happy, though it makes me suffer.

ALBERTUS: Explain this mystery to me.

HANZ: Master, love makes me better. It raises my soul, it sets it on fire, and I feel myself closer to God when I feel myself lover and poet . . . But let us return, Master; the rain increases, and the road will be difficult. You seem more tired than usual.

ALBERTUS: Hanz, I feel weak . . . I believe I have lost heart.

ACT FOUR

The Strings of Steel

Scene One

On the great tower of the cathedral. [The massive stone tower is topped by a flat roof or terrace, with parapets. From the center of the terrace rises a conical spire, perhaps another thirty or forty feet in height, topped by a gilded bronze statue of an archangel, blowing a trumpet. On opposite sides of the spire two ladders are affixed to it, giving access to the base of the statue.]

ALBERTUS: Let's stop on this terrace, my child. This rapid climb must have exhausted your strength.

HELEN: No. I can climb higher, higher and higher.

ALBERTUS: You cannot climb the spire of the cathedral. The ladder is dangerous and the fresh air that blows here is already exciting enough for you.

HELEN: I want to climb, always to climb, to climb until I recover the lyre. A wicked spirit has snatched it up and carried it to the point of the spire. He has set it in the arms of the golden archangel that shines in the sun. But I shall go to find it; I fear nothing. The lyre is calling me. (*She starts to bound up the ladder.*)

ALBERTUS, *restraining her*: Stop, my dear Helen. Your delirium misleads you. The lyre has by no means been snatched away. It is I who took it from your bedside table to prevent you from playing it. But come home and I shall return it.

HELEN: No, no! You and the Jew Jonathas have an agreement to torment the lyre and do me to death. The Jew has carried it up there. I am going to recover it. Follow me, if you dare. (*She begins to climb the ladder.*)

ALBERTUS, *showing her the lyre, which he is carrying under his coat*: Helen, Helen! Here it is. Look at it! In the name of heaven, return. I'll let you play it all you want. But come back down the steps or you are going to perish.

HELEN, *stopping*: Give me the lyre and fear nothing.

ALBERTUS: No! I shall give it to you here. Come back. Oh, heavens! I don't dare climb after her. I'm afraid that in her haste or in seeking to struggle, she may fall from the tower.

HELEN: Master, extend your arm and give me the lyre, or I shall never descend this ladder.

ALBERTUS, *holding the lyre up to her*: All right, all right, Helen. Take it. And now lean on my arm; come down carefully. (*Helen seizes the lyre and climbs the ladder rapidly toward the top of the spire.*)

ALBERTUS, *following her part way up*: Oh, heavens, heavens! She is lost; she's going to fall. Unhappy man, what good have your precautions done? They have only served to hasten her doom. (*To Hanz and Wilhelm, who arrive on the terrace*) O my friends, my children! See the peril to which she is exposed. . . . [*He descends to the terrace.*]

HELEN: Leave me alone. If one of you puts a foot on the steps I throw myself down.

WILHELM: The wisest course is to let her indulge her fantasy. By wanting to save her we only ensure her death.

HANZ: Do not fear, Master. There is in her a spirit that possesses her. She acts by a supernatural impulse. Leave her alone; say nothing to her. I'm going to climb up the opposite ladder without her seeing me. I shall hide behind the bronze archangel, and if she is intent on jumping I shall throw myself on her and hold her by force. Act as though you were not worried about her. (*He goes around the spire and mounts the ladder on the opposite side. Albertus and Wilhelm lean on the parapet of the tower. Helen, at the top of the spire, sits on the step at the feet of the statue of the archangel.*)

ALBERTUS: What a terrifying spectacle! Can she keep from becoming dizzy, suspended in midair, without support, without a railing, on the narrow base? Oh, miserable that I am! I shall be the cause of her death.

WILHELM: Master, her very delirium makes her unaffected by dizziness. She will escape danger because she has no awareness of it. Moreover, see! Hanz is already near her, behind the statue. Hanz is vigorous and intrepid. He is calm in crisis. He will save her. Take courage, and above all, keep calm. (*Helen tunes the lyre.*)

ALBERTUS, *aside*: If she perceives the loss of the two strings, who knows what act of despair she could take! But no! . . . She doesn't realize it . . . She is dreaming. She is inspired by the spectacle spread out beneath her feet!

SPIRIT OF THE LYRE: O daughter of men! You see this dazzling spectacle. Hear these powerful harmonies.

HELEN: I see nothing but a sea of glowing dust here and there pierced by masses of lead-colored roofs and domes of reddish copper, where the sun darts its burning rays. I hear nothing but a confused clamor, like the humming of an immense beehive, punctuated momentarily by sharp cries and mournful groans.

SPIRIT OF THE LYRE: What you see is the empire of man; what you hear is the soughing of the human race.

HELEN: Now I see and hear better. My eyes pierce the moving clouds and distinguish men's movements and actions. My ears grow accustomed to this muffled clamor and sense the discourse and noise of the human race.

SPIRIT OF THE LYRE: Isn't it a magic picture and a striking concert? See the grandeur and power of man! Admire his riches, so dearly won, and the marvels of his tireless industry. See the majestic temples that, like giants, raise their haughty heads above the numberless mass of elegant or modest homes squatting at their feet. See the resplendent cupolas, like silver mirrors, tapering obelisques, slender colonnades, palaces of marble, where through every crystal window the sun illuminates thousand-faceted diamonds. Look upon this river that coils, like a serpent of gold and azure, around the flanks of the great city, while bridges of iron and granite—some lined with white statues that are reflected in the waves, others hung as if by magic on invisible strands of metal—leap from one bank to the other, sometimes in arches of strong and massive stone, sometimes in webs of transparent and delicate ironwork, and sometimes in elastic gangways that bend without breaking under the weight of carriages and horsemen.[39] See triumphant arches, where jasper and porphyry, worked by the most skilled hands, supply the pedestal for statues of great men or trophies of war. See everywhere symbols of

39. The description of the city, which closely resembles Paris, may have been suggested by the description of the view from the top of Notre-Dame in Victor Hugo's *Notre-Dame de Paris*, book 3, chapter 2.

power and genius, pediments covered with emblems, Victories with outstretched wings, horses of bronze that seem to frisk under the hand of conquerors. See splaying fountains, constructions where science accomplishes its wonders; museums where art piles up its masterpieces; theaters where, every day, imagination sees its most beautiful dreams realized. See, too, immense roadsteads where the flags of all nations float under a forest of masts and where, from the ends of the earth, commerce comes to exchange its riches. Turn your gaze afar. See fertile villages, fecund plains sowed with magnificent villas and cut in all directions by great roads planted with trees, where carriages fly through the dust and where the pavement is scorched under the feet of rapid coursers. See marvels still more grand: on narrow paths, rails of iron, that sometimes raise themselves over the hills and sometimes dive down and are lost in the bosom of the earth, you see roll, with the speed of lightning, heavy carriages coupled in a train that carry whole populations from one frontier to another in the space of a day and that have for motive power only a column of black smoke. Could we not speak of the chariot of Vulcan, rolled by the formidable hand of invisible cyclopses? See also on the waters the power of this vapor that furrows the surface of the sea by means of fiery paddle wheels and makes it docile, like the plain to the slicing of the plow.

And now hear! These myriads of terrible or sublime harmonies are confused in a single roar, a thousand times more powerful than that of the tempest: this is the voice of industry, the noise of machines, the hissing of steam, and the blow of hammers, the rolling of drums, the fanfare of military phalanxes, the declamation of orators, the melodies of a thousand different instruments, cries of joy, of war and of work, the hymn of triumph and of might. Hear and rejoice, for this world is rich and this race ingenious and powerful.

WILHELM: Master, the hour and the place inspire Helen. The lyre has never been more sonorous, the song never more masculine,[40] and the harmony never more grand or knowledgeable.

ALBERTUS: Yes, now at last I understand the language of the lyre. Life surges in my blood and kindles my brain with the fire of enthusiasm. I seem to see beyond the limit of the horizon and to hear the voice of all peoples married to an eloquent voice emanating from my own breast.

WILHELM: Now Helen touches the lyre. Doubtless the nature of our emotion is going to change. Listen carefully!

HELEN, *playing the lyre*: O Spirit! Where have you brought me? Why have you chained me to this place, to force me to see and hear what fills my eyes with tears and my heart with bitterness? I see below me only the immeasurable depths of despair and hear only the howlings of grief without resource and without end! This world is a sea of blood, an ocean of tears. What I see is not one city; I see ten, a hundred, a thousand, all the cities of the earth. Not one province, but a country, a continent, a world, all the entire earth. I see it suffer and I hear it groan. Everywhere cadavers and around them groans. My God, what corpses! My God, what groans! . . .

Oh, what livid dying, couched on a diseased pallet! What criminals and innocents, agonizing pell-mell on the damp stone of a dungeon! What unfortunates, crushed under heavy burdens or bent under thankless work! I see children who swim in filth, women who laugh and dance in filth, sumptuous beds, splendid tables covered with filth, men in purple and ermine coats stained with filth, entire peoples lying in filth. The earth is only a mass of filth worked by rivers of

40. With the masculine view of technology expressed by the Spirit, compare the feminine view of suffering soon expressed by Helen.

blood. I see battlefields covered with smoking corpses and scattered limbs still palpitating, or others where ponderous battalions rush headlong to the sound of the trumpets of war. I clearly see arms glitter in the sun; I hear well the songs of hope and triumph. But I hear also the groans of the wounded, the last sighs of the dying whom the hoofs of horses trample. I hear too the cry of vultures and ravens that strut between the armies, and the air is darkened by their sinister flight. They alone will be the vanquishers. They alone will intone tonight the hymn of triumph, while thrusting their bloody claws into the flesh of victims.

I see palaces, armies, festivals, extravagance, noisy celebration. I see and hear gold rustle on tables and in coffers. These are the tears of the poor, the sweat of workmen, the blood of soldiers that swills over these tables and is locked in coffers . . . Each coin should be struck with an effigy of a man of the people, for every one of these pieces of metal has cost the health, honor, or life of a man of the people.

I see monarchs seated on their lofty thrones, around whom the nations prostrate themselves and whom a triple brazen rampart of armies guards. But I hear also those who threaten and those who weep at the palace gates; I hear the trees of the royal gardens fall to the axe and the pavement piled with corpses to block the march of bloody soldiers. I hear the cries of riot, the noble hymn of deliverance, the noise of cannons, the creaking of buildings that fall on conquered and vanquishers alike; I hear the terrible tocsin that shakes old towers and sounds in panting breath victory and funerals.

I hear too the sonorous speech of numerous orators; I hear lying and blasphemy stifle the word of justice; I hear the unruly applause of the crowd that carries informers and forgers in triumph.

I see majestic assemblies and hear what is discussed there. Some say the question is one of relieving the misery of the people. The rest reply the people are too rich, too happy, too powerful. I hear the immense mass of pharisees who raise themselves slowly while saying in a somber tone, "Let him perish!" And I see the powers of the earth who perfume their hands while saying, a smile upon their lips, "Let him perish!"

ALBERTUS: The rhythm is lugubrious and the melody heart-rending. See how Helen suffers, how her face is pale and how her arms are twisted despairingly around the lyre. O unhappy priestess! I wanted to be initiated by you into the poetry of civilization. Pythoness[41] chained to the tripod, you expiate in these tortures my criminal curiosity. O Helen, cease your song, come back to us! . . .

WILHELM: Master, Hanz has made us a sign not to call to her. Ravished in a painful ecstasy, she forgets that we hear her. The danger is she may awaken and that dizziness may overtake her.

SPIRIT OF THE LYRE: Daughter of men, why do you so despair? Have you forgotten Providence? Is it not she who permits these things to lead all men, by harsh experience and slow expiation, to knowledge of the truth and to love of justice? Look, there are already some pious men and some truly pure hearts. Does not the crime of the one bring about the virtue of the others? Does not the iniquity of tyrants create as a counterpart the patience or daring of the oppressed? See! What sublime self-sacrifice, what courageous efforts, what evangelic resignation! See these closed and patient hands that fortify themselves for deliverance while, to encourage them, captives stifle their groans behind the bars of the prison. See these friends who embrace. Do you not perceive the last hug of one who accompanies another to the foot of the scaffold?

41. Priestess of the Greek oracle at Delphi.

Do you take in the last look of one who, while smiling, places his head under the axe?

HELEN: I see violated virgins and butchered children; I see old folk hung from the gibbet; I see a woman dragged by courtesans to the bed of a prince, there expiring in his arms of shame and despair. I see her husband receiving gold and honors in return for his silence and kissing the hand of the prince. I see a young woman, beaten with rods in the public square by soldiers for having sung "No, the nation is not lost!" And she goes mad. I see children separated from their mother, isolated from their family, taught to curse their father's name and to disown the heroism of their blood! I see heroes proscribed, liberators on whose head a price is set; I see young martyrs dragged out of prison because they did not die quickly enough and carried to the icy north for fear their last sighs may pierce the walls of the dungeon and reach the ears of their brothers. I see peasants whose flesh is torn with iron hooks because they forgot to cut their beards and to don the livery of the conqueror. I see a nation erased from the face of the globe as if it had never existed. They deprive it of its leaders, its liberators, its priests, its institutions, its goods, its costume, and even its name, that it may perish utterly; and the world looks on, saying "Let it perish!"

SPIRIT OF THE LYRE: You see the evil that is shown; you see not the good that is hidden. Can you not read in the depths of generous souls who prepare the day of justice? Don't you hear the prayer of exiles and the songs for the lost homeland that call down the anger of heaven on the unjust, pity for the weak, protection for the strong? Daughter of the lyre, instead of lamenting the crimes and misfortunes of man, kneel down and invoke help from above. Let us pray together, let us join our tears and our prayers! Let us pray! May our love give us hope and strength! Let us pray! Let us hold ourselves in an embrace, prostrate at the feet of one who. . . .

HELEN: Be silent! Don't name that which does not exist! If a fatal power presides over the destinies of humanity, it is the demon of evil, for impunity protects crime. Why do you talk of Providence? Why of love? Providence is mute, deaf, impotent for these victims. It is clever and active in serving the designs of the perverse. Curses on you, O Providence! And on you, Spirit! Do not speak to me any more. You have revealed to me the wickedness of which I was ignorant: let my silence be punishment for your cruel instruction. Seek love in a heart you have not crushed. Ask your safety of a soul that can still love and believe.[42] (*She raises herself up. Albertus makes a cry.*)

WILHELM: No, no! She does not want to make an attempt on her life. See! She is throwing the lyre to the ground and descends toward us as lightly as a swallow who hides her nest in the top of an old tower. Oh, how beautiful she is with her scattered hair and her white dress undulating in the wind!

HELEN, *throwing herself into the arms of Albertus*: My father, take me away, hide me! Take me down into the darkness of the earth. I don't want to see the sun; I don't want to hear any human noise. Let no one speak to me . . . I want to pluck out my eyes, to be buried in the ground like a mole, asleep like a chrysalis.

ALBERTUS: Helen, take yourself away from me, turn your hatred upon me, I am author of all your misfortunes . . . I wanted to deprive you of the lyre . . .

---

42. Some of what is said here reflects the disillusionment of Sand and her friends when the "July Revolution" of 1830 had not led to a socialist republic.

HELEN: Don't speak to me more of the lyre. The lyre is broken. I have thrown it to the wind . . . We will not see it again . . . Hanz, my friend, take me away . . . This place gives me the dizziness of despair.

ALBERTUS: Take her away quickly, my boys. I will follow you.

Scene Two

In the public square. A group of merchants.

A MERCHANT: The music has stopped. Truly it is a wonderful thing and its like has not been heard by man.

SECOND MERCHANT: What are you making such a fuss about, neighbor? Has the price of sugar gone down again?

AN OLD WOMAN: A miracle, sir, a veritable miracle!

SECOND MERCHANT: The café isn't paying any more taxes?

THE WOMAN: No, sir, the archangel on the cathedral has played the trumpet.

THIRD MERCHANT: What archangel? What trumpet?

FIRST MERCHANT: *Parbleu*, pal! The copper archangel that is up there, up there, and that's been blowing into his trumpet since the time of King Dagobert[43] without making even the littlest sound. Well, just now he played some charming airs for more than twenty minutes. I heard it as. . . .

SECOND MERCHANT: As you hear me talk when I say nothing. Tell it to the marines, Spiegendorf!

---

43. King of the Franks, A.D. 628–39.

THIRD MERCHANT: It's all in your imagination, my good woman. Your ears are burning.[44]

THE WOMAN: Sir, I am not that kind of a woman.

SECOND MERCHANT: If that's all you've got to say, it was hardly worth my while to stir out of my counting house.

THIRD MERCHANT: That's what I think too. I saw these nincompoops collected there in the middle of the square, staring at the tips of their upturned noses that they mistook for the spire of the cathedral. I was hoping . . . that is, I thought that someone had fallen from the top of the tower and I came quickly to see.

SECOND MERCHANT: They probably heard the organist of the cathedral practicing the air "Mary, sop your bread"[45] to play for us Sunday at high mass.

FIRST MERCHANT: Well, probably that's what it was.

THE WOMAN: I know the sound of the organ very well. Moreover, the church is closed. There's no sound from there. And then the angel did not at all play church tunes. It's very odd how unreligious it was.

FIRST MERCHANT: But it was pretty, very pretty!

THIRD MERCHANT: Perhaps they have invented some musical contraption that they've stowed in the body of the statue so that it has the appearance of playing the trumpet. I bet it's going to strike all the hours, like the clock of Jean de Nivelle.

44. That is, someone is gossiping about her.
45. A well-known French rhyme: "Marie, trempe ton pain, Marie, trempe ton pain, Marie, trempe ton pain, dans la sauce! Marie, trempe ton pain, Marie, trempe ton pain, Marie, trempe ton pain, dans le vin!" and so on.

SECOND MERCHANT: Or more likely only at midday. What time is it?

FIRST MERCHANT: It is certain that there was something white at the feet of the statue.

THIRD MERCHANT: That's it. It was a dial-plate.

FIRST MERCHANT: It doesn't matter, I'm going to see what's there. I know the concierge of the towers. He will let me go up.

THIRD MERCHANT: All right, I'm going too. (*The two depart.*)

THE WOMAN: As for me, I'm going to tell the whole town what I heard. (*She leaves.*)

SECOND MERCHANT, *with an air of assurance, crossing his arms over his apron*: Could one believe that there are still so many superstitious people today? . . . Ah, there's Master Albertus coming by here. He's a man I do not like to meet. He looks at you in a droll way, and things go on in his house that even the devil doesn't understand. Oh, the Jew Jonathas Taer is coming after him! . . . This time I'm going home. I don't at all like people who run through the streets after their death.[46] (*He flees.*)

Scene Three

Enter Albertus and Mephistopheles.

MEPHISTOPHELES, *following Albertus, who does not see him*: Where are you rushing so eagerly and nervously, my respectable master? You don't have a glance, not even a simple nod of the head for your best friend this morning.

46. In act 2, scene 3, Mephistopheles mentions reports of Taer's death at Hamburg.

ALBERTUS: Always that Jew! He follows me like remorse . . . Leave me alone, sir, please! I do not have the honor of being your friend and I have no time to waste.

MEPH., *still following him and now coming close to him*: I understand your distress. Helen's condition upsets you. But be assured, she has never been in better health.

ALBERTUS, *shrugging his shoulders*: What do you know of it?

MEPH.: You can't doubt that I know a lot more about many things than you.

ALBERTUS: Keep your damned knowledge. It has only cost me trouble and worry.

MEPH.: I am astonished that such a great philosopher is disheartened by a little trouble. Don't you teach every day in your lectures that it is necessary to suffer much in order to arrive at the truth? That one cannot pay too dearly for conquest of truth? That truth is only bought at the price of sweat, tears, and even blood? . . .

ALBERTUS: Ever since I listened to you I have suffered much, and far from having arrived at the truth, it seems to me I am further removed from it than ever. Helen's mental disturbance increases, and nothing explains to me the sympathetic properties of the lyre.

MEPH.: Permit me to differ. First, the delirium of Helen is not increasing. Yesterday, all day long, after her walk along the stream, she was filled with reason.

ALBERTUS: It is true that her delirium only began at the moment when I refused her the lyre. Then she bolted out of the house and I could only catch up with her on the top of the great tower.

MEPH.: Moreover, why did you want to prevent her from making the lyre play?

ALBERTUS: I feared just what happened. When I saw her so sensible and following with such clarity a very abstract lesson that I had just given her, I deceived myself into thinking she was cured, and I wanted the lyre to be destroyed. For, do not doubt it, all her madness comes from that instrument.

MEPH.: Without doubt. You have always regarded what is a very certain fact as though it were a story, a reverie of old Meinbaker. The first attack of madness and the long sickness that followed had no cause other than the touching of the lyre.

ALBERTUS: The fact has been well proved for me today. But let it remain a mystery. I shall not torment myself with it any more. Helen could perish, victim of my curiosity. Thank God she escaped today from her most recent danger. The lyre is destroyed. She threw it from the height of the tower onto the marble pavement.

MEPH.: That doesn't prevent it from being intact. You will find it on the pedestal in your study. It only lacks the strings you yourself removed, and the sound box is not even cracked. The carved figures have lost neither arms nor limbs in the accident, and I am sure that the tune has not been adversely affected at all.

ALBERTUS: What you say is impossible. You are making fun of me, but I give you notice I am tired of your talk.

MEPH.: Never speak to me again if the lyre is not as I say and where I say. It fell at my feet, while I was listening to Helen at the bottom of the great tower, and at that moment I saw your governess Therese pass. I told her to pick it up and carry it home.

ALBERTUS: I'll soon know what to believe. But how could you hear the lyre at so great a distance?

MEPH.: The sound of the lyre has that peculiar quality that, however soft it is, one can hear the least notes from one end of the town to another. The whole district heard it today. As for me, my ears are very sharp, and I could repeat to you word for word what the lyre and Helen said to each other on the high peak of the bell tower.

ALBERTUS: You understand then the meaning of the music perfectly?

MEPH.: Very well indeed. Did it not sing today of the marvels and miseries of civilization? While the lyre spoke of the grandeur and genius of man, did Helen not speak of man's crimes and misfortunes?

ALBERTUS: Yes, I understood that too—all right for this time, to my great surprise. The manuscript of Adelsfreit predicted it.

MEPH.: "On three strings the melody will be strong and clear. All will comprehend it, for the two strings of steel treat of man, his inventions, his laws, and his morals." You see that I have Adelsfreit's words on the tip of my tongue. As for the brazen string, the last of all. . . . "he who makes it vibrate will know the mystery of the lyre."

ALBERTUS: Well I don't know that. I reject it. I shall break up the lyre when I return home.

MEPH.: You are presumptuous. Do you believe that is in your power? The lyre has just fallen to the ground without receiving the slightest damage. Your hand would be broken while trying to destroy it.

ALBERTUS: How does it happen then that I break the delicate strings without wanting to and with the lightest touch?

MEPH.: All that is part of the mystery you don't want to know. Have you never heard it asserted that a poetic and tender soul bravely resists the reversal of fortune, while it is grieved, constrained, and crushed by the slightest check to its affections? You yourself smiled when brutal authority closed your lectures and stopped your publications. Yet if Helen is sick or if one of your students commits an act of ingratitude against you, your strength is vanquished and you shed tears like a baby. The mystery of the lyre is no more inexplicable than that.

ALBERTUS: You get yourself off the hook by comparisons and symbols.

MEPH.: Everything is symbol in the intellectual realm as in the material. These two levels obey analogous laws and fulfill analogous phenomena. In starting from this reasoning and in breaking again two strings of the lyre you will get hold of the secret.

ALBERTUS: I will not do it. God knows what crisis Helen would have to undergo this time.

MEPH.: It is a noble sacrifice, and I approve of your attitude. However, I am sorry to say that all this has made much noise and that the whole country is convulsed with stories of sorcerers and ghosts, occasioned by the madness of Helen and the strange sound of the lyre. You pass now for a magician, and I too by association with you. You know that I am quite willing to laugh at all these things as they concern me, but as for you, I am truly distressed to see you lose all your salutary influence, and I foresee that your excellent teachings, far from bearing fruit, are going to fall into complete discredit.

ALBERTUS: Don't try to control me by vanity. I am indifferent to what men will say of me.

MEPH.: It's not a question of that. You had a mission to fill among men, and you are abandoning them to ignorance and error . . .

ALBERTUS: I don't love humanity enough to sacrifice Helen to it. Helen is a pure soul, a celestial being. Men are all despots, traitors, or brutes.

MEPH.: I see that the music has had some effect. It's the characteristic of the lyre to impose on those who hear it the emotions of the one who makes it speak. It would be very unfortunate for you to remain under this false impression; the world would lose much thereby and you may come to feel great remorse.

ALBERTUS: Aren't you the one who involved me in the destruction of the strings which could have, by their melody, raised and inflamed my soul? It well suits you to reproach me with the result of your advice!

MEPH.: You will thank me for my advice when you have completed your task, that is to say when you have made the lyre an instrument of one string. Think of this again in a symbolic way. To elevate your soul toward the ideal as you have succeeded in doing, have you not, for many years now, worked to crush in your own breast the nerves which thrill at terrestrial joys? Have you not destroyed everything that could distract you from your goal, and have you not concentrated all your thought, all your sentiments, all your instincts on a single object?

ALBERTUS: That's true, but here I am working at cross purposes. I began by destroying in the lyre the poetry of the infinite, and I have arrived at the poetry of terrestrial things, while, in my own philosophical work, I have proceeded in the opposite direction.

MEPH.: You have made a mistake. What one stifles before its birth is never really dead. Needs suppressed before their development imperiously demand their life. That's what has happened to you. Your virtue has made you the most un-happy man in the world and at the present time, while every day preaching certainty, you do not possess it on any point.

ALBERTUS, *aside*: I am terrified at seeing this man read me in this way.

MEPH.: If you rest there, you are lost, my good friend. You must return to faith by a strong reaction. You must know the passions, their anguish, their perils, even their fury. You must, in a word, pass through the trial of fire; as a result, you will give testimony of your faith, for you will have known life, and you will no longer be deceived.

ALBERTUS: You give me hateful advice. Do you believe that the human soul is so mad as to stand up to such a trial? That is to tempt God by abandoning oneself to the evil of the gaiety of the heart. Whoever tests his strength in this way will pay dearly and will lose the feeling and desire for the ideal in the exercise of evil instincts.

MEPH.: Who is talking about doing evil and cultivating gross instincts? You are forgetting that I am as much a philosopher as you, although I am not so licensed. I'm not advising you to degrade yourself, but to renew yourself. There is one grand passion, grand in its childishness, generous in its transports, sublime in its delirium: that is love. You were misled when you believed that your ideal could absorb all the flame in your breast. This flame is of two sorts: one is for the heavens, the other for the earth. And one can no more devour the other than human will can stifle either. (*Putting his hand on Albertus's arm*) Who knows better than you, my dear philosopher? This earthly flame consumes you, and nothing has been able to extinguish it in you!

ALBERTUS, *trembling and speaking to himself*: His words inflame my blood, and yet my hand is as cold as marble!

MEPH., *continuing to hold his hand*: Give food to this flame, and when it has burned for the needed time it will extinguish itself. Being of earthly nature, it should perish. The other, which is celestial, will survive it and will possess you entirely.

ALBERTUS: But to love it is necessary to be loved.

MEPH.: Perhaps you are already, without your suspecting it.

ALBERTUS: I? . . . Who could then be loving me? . . . (*Brusquely*) Master Jonathas, do not name her! . . . I forbid it.

MEPH.: You think her name would be profaned in my mouth? You are already quite amorous, Master Albertus?

ALBERTUS, *troubled*: But she loves me not; she will never love me . . .

MEPH.: She will love you when you want her to, and this love will restore her reason, health, and life!

ALBERTUS: What then must be done so that she will love me?

MEPH.: It is necessary to break two more strings of the lyre. And when you are tired of loving, or distressed by the force of your love, it will only remain for you to be cured of it at once.

ALBERTUS: How is that?

MEPH.: By marrying Helen and breaking the last string of the lyre! (*Aside*) He is mine! (*He disappears.*)

ALBERTUS, *in a sort of bewilderment*: God! How cold is the imprint of his hand! . . . My sight is troubled . . . I have difficulty finding my way . . . Could it be that the lyre was not crushed? . . .

ACT FIVE

The Brazen String

Scene One

Albertus, in his study, contemplating the lyre; Mephistopheles, invisible to him, seated in a corner.

MEPHISTOPHELES, *aside*: That's it! Contemplate your drudgery, groan, work yourself into a fright, strike your breast. That will change nothing, and you can play at your ease now on the one string that remains. It will be pretty music, but unfortunately, it will not last for long!

ALBERTUS: I haven't been able to resist![47] . . . What then is this infernal temptation? That damned Jew, with his manuscripts and his advice, has made a child of me. He has overthrown my reason by holding out to me a secret that I doubtless will never know! . . . I vainly seek in these papers what song is assigned to the seventh string. Adelsfreit did not explain himself at all on this subject, and I have been forced to take myself back to Jonathas. Incomprehensible predictions! You have yet been realized with a completeness by which a greater knowledge of science than mine would be frightened. But the more impenetrable the mystery seems, the more my conscience must seek an explanation. I owe the solution to men, I owe it to myself. Without it, their spirit and mine could remain forever frustrated. Men! My conscience! Is it then for them, is it for it that I have tried the experiment? Is it love of

47. In the interval between acts 4 and 5, Albertus has broken the steel strings.

the truth that has guided me in all this? Is that what devours me at this moment? Ah, wretch, admit that in breaking these two strings what has taken control of you is a mad love of life, a burning thirst of passions. Oh! How my hand trembled, how my heart was on fire when I followed the Jew's advice! I kept expecting to see the sky darkened, the earth tremble, and my house fall in upon me. Nothing of that sort happened, and I did not even hear the strings of steel give a plaintive sound as did the others I have broken. This time the lyre was silent! Perhaps it is my conscience that has become deaf! . . . But what then is my crime? If the action is useful in itself, what difference does it make that an evil intention crept in among the good, in spite of myself? I had to follow here the truth through the evidence. And even if the peace of my soul may be forever troubled at it, still it is a sacrifice I owe to my work.

MEPH., *showing himself in the figure of the Jew*: A thousand pardons if I interrupt without ceremony the secret of your thoughts. Great spirits have the bad habit of talking aloud with themselves. That wouldn't happen to you if you knew music, but you are not delaying to know it, for I find you engaged in the greatest ideas. It seems to me that you begin to open your eyes and to recognize that you ought to feel the pulse of life if you want to be the true physician of humanity.

ALBERTUS, *aside*: This man annoys me. I distrust him and yet he leads me where he wishes. Why is it that his visit is agreeable to me at this instant? Could it be that I need a worse conscience than my own to encourage me in evil?

MEPH.: You wouldn't be a monk, by any chance?

ALBERTUS: Nothing annoys me to a greater extent than this joking. What are you trying to say?

MEPH.: That you call a crime everything that is outside of your personal morality.

ALBERTUS: If so, am I not right at least in my own case? All is relative.

MEPH.: I express myself badly. I ought to have said "mad desire," "rash pride."

ALBERTUS: This reproach is trite. Since you pretend to read within me, you ought to know that my renunciation of human things is a simple and conscientious resolution.

MEPH.: As you please. I would rather pass for proud than for a nincompoop.

ALBERTUS: Your mistake and irony do not affect me at all.

MEPH.: That means you're offended. Come on, let's not quarrel. For the last twenty-five years you have been the victim of an error, that's all. It is time to free yourself of it. You've thought that a philosopher ought to be a saint. Instead of seeking sanctity in the well-directed employment of your faculties, you have followed the old routine of bigots in trying to extinguish the same faculties. What ought to lead you to recognize your illusion is that you ought to remember the doubts that tortured your soul ever since the day you entered on this career up to now. Moreover, these faculties have only grown and constantly demanded their employment. The master you invoke, and with whom you believe yourself in direct rapport, would be very ungrateful and very foolish not to help you if, while sacrificing yourself in this way, you had fulfilled his intentions. Learn to recognize, in the revolt of the needs of your heart, the legitimacy of these needs, or else doubt this celestial power you are always calling to witness and to which you offer all your sacrifices. Let's see. What mission do you believe you are engaged in now? Is it to attain your salvation as a monk, or to seek wisdom in order to teach it to men as a philosopher? If the latter, learn that one does not teach what one does not know. The wisdom you are practicing is an exceptional state that can formulate everything for two or three followers, placed like you on a unique path. It is a work of fantasy that exhibits itself in a series of artistic attempts. You always demand that poets give an accounting of the morality and utility of their works, but you would be hard put to prove how your celibacy can be profitable to society.

ALBERTUS: Yet you cannot deny that I have taught some useful truths, and I shall reply that I would not have had the leisure to discover and teach these truths if I had lived my life at the caprice of the passions.

MEPH.: Who is talking about caprices or passions? Couldn't you cultivate, in the sanctuary of your soul, as you put it, a pure love, conjugal bliss, lasting and legitimate? Couldn't you have married, been a father? Then you would have taught with authority the duties of the family of which you speak so often to your students, rather the way a blind man speaks of colors.

ALBERTUS: I have often dreamed of it, but I felt in my soul the germ of passions so violent that I could not give to marriage such a calm, such a noble, such a lasting role as my reason conceived for it and as my conviction preached to others.

MEPH.: And why, please, has the germ of your passions become so burning and so dangerous? It is because you have compromised it too long. Thus, with all your virtue, you are inferior to the least citizen of your city.

ALBERTUS: I am only too convinced. But the evil is done. The more I have delayed, the more certain it is that I must not enter into this way of life. There are perhaps some errors in which wisdom ordains that we preserve an appearance, or at least condemns us to carry the burden to the end.

MEPH.: That's the prettiest sophism that ever came from the mouth of a sage. But none the less, it is a well-established sophism. Say plainly that what stops you today is timidity: on the one hand, the fear of not knowing how to please a woman; on the other, the fear of seeming ridiculous to your students.

ALBERTUS: I can swear before God and before men that you are mistaken. If I believed I would become better and more useful to society by marrying, I would do it immediately, with simplicity, with boldness. I think well enough of women to believe that among them would be found at least one who would be touched by my candor, and I know my students well enough to be sure they would appreciate my good faith. But I am certain that love would be thereafter a poison to my soul. I would be carried on to involve myself so much in the love of a creature like myself that I would lose the feeling for the in-finite and diligent contemplation of divinity. Jealousy would devour my entrails and would little by little destroy all my ideas of justice, patience, and abnegation. In return for the children I should give to the fatherland, I would withdraw my teaching, which is certainly more necessary to the state. Arms are always less lacking than intelligence. Is not that your opinion?

MEPH.: So you have firmly decided to remain a monk. That's your last word?

ALBERTUS: If that is the way you want to describe me, so be it! It is my final resolution.

MEPH.: In that case, tell me, Master Albertus, why you re-duced the lyre to this single brazen string.

ALBERTUS, *troubled*: What does the sound of this lyre and the physical experiences of which it is the source have in common with my conduct and the sentiments of my soul?

MEPH.: What does poetry have in common with love: That's something that never came to the attention of a philosopher!

ALBERTUS: That's enough. Your railleries tire me, and what I have just been saying to you is sad enough to merit from you something other than cold disdain. You are a man without a heart. Leave me!

MEPH.: You accuse me ungratefully when I am helping you despite yourself. You are the dupe of your own sophisms. You had put some invincible obstacles between yourself and happiness, the restraint and gaucherie of a philosopher! I made you understand and modify the magic properties of this lyre. Thanks to me, you have in your hands a magic object with which you can touch the heart of Helen and appear to her younger and more handsome than the youngest and most beautiful of your students . . . And you disdain it, to reinforce yourself in your stupid pride or your cowardly prudence. All right, let your destiny be accomplished. For now, the melody of the lyre is so simplified that you could play it as well as Helen and act upon her as until now she has acted upon you . . . The tender Wilhelm or the passionate Hanz or the handsome Carl will play in your place. And Helen, cured forever of her madness, will be the happy and chaste wife of the one of the three who most inspires her! . . . Good night, Master, I wish you a good evening and long days on the earth!

ALBERTUS: Wait. What are you saying?!!! Helen cured? Helen happy?

MEPH.: My company tires you. Adieu!

ALBERTUS: One word more! Do you have such faith in the incomprehensible power of this magical object that you dare to promise me comparable results? Adelsfreit's manuscript breaks off at the brazen string.

MEPH.: Since when do you join faith to sorcery? Don't you see that it is all a game? When you believed Helen was playing the lyre with her mind you had before your eyes a film that kept you from making out the actions of her hands. When the brook was stopped at her order, the miller closed the sluice. When the lyre fell from the top of the cathedral to the pavement, a raven seized it in its fall and deposited it gently on the ground. Everything is explained by natural facts. I don't believe in breaking one's head in seeking the meaning of an enigma when the first explanation coming is as good as all the others. Good night, Master, for the last time! (*He makes himself invisible to Albertus, and remains near him, leaning on the back of his armchair.*)

ALBERTUS: No! All this was not explicable as accidents. The miracles accomplished by the lyre can still be accomplished, and every day we receive from heaven blessings that pass the limit of our intelligence. Perhaps it has been reserved for me to give happiness and receive it by imparting to the lyre an unknown eloquence and a sympathetic power. Oh, to restore reason to Helen, and in return to be loved by her! (*Seizing the lyre.*) O lyre, is it possible you could perform such a miracle and that your last string, docile at last under my unskilled fingers, might reveal to me poetry, grace, enthusiasm, and all the powers of seduction? When you vibrate under my hand, will a flame descend from on high to illuminate my brow and to reveal to me this language of the infinite that Helen speaks and that I hardly understand? Yes, without doubt, as a poet and musician, invested with this magic without which the world is cold and dark, I shall know how to make love. I will no longer be the sad philosopher whose appearance only inspires fear and whose speech only boredom. Sullen envelope, uncouth gravity, I am going to strip you off like the clothes of yesterday in the rays of the springtime . . . Oh, I am overwhelmed! The hope of being happy has taken from me the hope of being good! Yes, I shall know how to love with justice, gentleness, confidence, for I shall know that I am loved in turn. And my friends will be happy at my good fortune, for I shall speak of it to them honestly, and they will see that my soul is sincere in joy as in suffering.

Scene Two

Helen, Albertus, Mephistopheles (invisible).

MEPHISTOPHELES, *aside*: Yes, Yes! Count on them, count on her, count on yourself! That's what I wait for. It does seem to me that despite his bragging, the Spirit of the Lyre is going to be chased out from there. Then Helen comes to me by right, and we will see how monsieur the philosopher will find conjugal love with the widow of an angel who has become mistress of the devil.

ALBERTUS, *looking at Helen, who is seated in a preoccupied attitude beside the window and pays no attention to him*: How pale and sad she is! Ah, her last song has crushed her! (*Approaching her*) Helen, you are sicker, my child? — She doesn't hear me, or doesn't want to reply. — Dear Helen, if you hear me, reply, if only with a look. Your silence distresses me, your indifference afflicts me. (*Helen looks at him with astonishment and casts her eyes out over the countryside.*)

ALBERTUS: Her reason is entirely gone. It would require a miracle to restore it. If I am the dupe of a gross impostor, pardon me, O Truth, O God! . . . For the first time, I am going to have recourse to something other than certainty. (*He tries the lyre, which remains silent.*)

MEPH., *aside*: Curses on you, incurable pedagogue! You can't even make the string of love resound! Who then will break the lyre? Let's go look for Hanz or Wilhelm. Perhaps they will be less crusty. What difference does it make, for that matter, who it is? Helen's purity cannot resist the charm of the brazen string, and whether she is defiled by the philosopher or by the whole town, still the Spirit of the Lyre will necessarily be humiliated and the philosopher be damned. (*He flies off.*)

Scene Three

ALBERTUS, *frantic*: All my efforts are in vain! It is mute to me, mute like Helen, mute like myself. And yet my soul is full of ardor and conviction! How is it then that for so long my lips have been closed and my tongue tied, like the voice in the breast of this instrument? Why have I never dared to say to Helen that I was in love with her? . . . Ah, the Jew has deceived me: he told me this magic object would give me the eloquence of love, and it is without effect in my hands. God punishes me for having believed in the power of chimeras by lifting my last illusion and by plunging me into the horror of despair. O solitude! I am always your prey. O desire! Insatiable vulture, of which my heart is the indestructible food! . . . (*He crosses his arms on his chest and looks at Helen with sadness. The lyre falls and gives a mighty sound. Helen trembles and rises.*)

HELEN: It is your voice! . . . Where then are you? (*She looks around her apprehensively, and after some efforts to recover memory, she perceives the lyre and seizes it with joy. The lyre resounds at once with force.*)

ALBERTUS: What deep and terrible sounds! . . . I was no longer believing in the power of the talisman. Yet this voice fills me with trouble and fear!

SPIRIT OF THE LYRE: The hour has come, O daughter of men! Now all my ties with the sky are broken. Now I belong to the earth. Now I am yours. Love me, O daughter of the lyre. Open your heart to me that I may dwell in it and cease to live in the lyre!

SPIRIT OF HELEN, *while Helen touches the brazen string*: Unknown being who has for so long spoken to me and who has never shown yourself to me, it seems to me that I love you, for I cannot love anything else on earth. But my love is sad and fear congeals it. I feel that your nature is superior to mine and I am afraid of sacrilege in loving an angel.

SPIRIT OF THE LYRE: If you wish to love me, O Helen, if you dare to take me and enclose me in your intelligence, I agree to lose myself there, to assimilate myself to it forever. Then we will be bound by an indissoluble marriage, and your spirit will see me face to face. O Helen, love me as I love you! Love is puissant, love is immense, love is all: it is love that is God; for love is the only thing that can be infinite in the heart of man.

SPIRIT OF HELEN: If love is God, it is eternal. Our marriage will then be eternal and my death will not break the bonds. Speak to me thus, if you wish that I love you, for the thirst for the infinite devours me, and I cannot conceive love without eternity!

CHOIR OF CELESTIAL SPIRITS: Let us draw near, let us encompass them, let us hover over their heads! Let the grace and power of God be here with us! The fatal hour approaches, the hour decisive for our young brother held captive in the lyre! Sweet spirit of harmony, may you see and hear us! But your ties with us are broken, the strings of gold and silver no longer call. Love alone brings us near to you. But terrestrial love drags you away and ravishes your memory. You no longer know us; your grievous trials are finished; your fate is in the hands of a daughter of men. May she remain faithful to the divine instincts that have preserved her until now from earthly love. O Powers of the heavens! Let us unite, let us inflame the air with the melodious beating of our wings!

ALBERTUS: See how she is transported into ecstasy, as though she heard divine language in the silence. Oh, how beautiful she is in this state! Yes, her soul is opened to the inspirations from the sky; her apparent madness is only the absence of the grosser instincts of life. Oh, charming creature, how often I have slandered you at other times when I doubted your intelligence! How often I have myself been a fool to defend me from the emotion your beauty inspired in me! It was a sacrilegious thought not to believe that such external beauty is bound to an intellectual beauty equally perfect. Helen, the powerful sounds that you have just made me hear have opened my soul to harmonies of the upper world. I sense that you celebrate the fires of a divine love, and this love penetrates my breast with a delicious hope. Hear me, for the soul is a lyre; and as you make it vibrate with your breath, you have awakened by your look a harmony hidden in the depth of my being . . . (*He kneels before Helen, who looks at him with surprise.*)

SPIRIT OF THE LYRE: Helen, Helen! A powerful spirit speaks to you, a spirit still bound to human life, but one whose flight already measures the heavens, a spirit of meditation, of analysis, and of knowledge . . . Helen, Helen, do not listen to him, for he is not, like you, a child of the lyre! . . . He is grand, he is just, he is in the light and in hope, but he has not yet lived in the love that the brazen string celebrates. Too much has he loved men, his brothers, to be absorbed in you. Helen, Helen, do not listen to him, but fear the language of wisdom. You have no need of wisdom, O daughter of the lyre! You have need only of love. Hear the voice that chants of love and not the voice that explains it.

ALBERTUS: Hear, hear, O Helen! Though daughter of poetry, you must hear my voice, for my voice comes from the depth of my heart, and true love cannot lack poetry, however austere its language. Let me tell you, young woman, that my heart desires you and that my intelligence needs yours. Man alone is incomplete. He is not truly man unless his thought has impregnated a soul in communion with his own. Do not fear your master, O my dear Helen! The master wants to become your disciple and to learn from you the secrets of the heavens. The plans of God are deep, and man can be initiated into them only by love. You who yesterday sang with so heart-rending a voice the crimes and misfortunes of humanity, know that blind and dissolute humanity wanders in the mud of the earth, like a flock without a shepherd. You know that it has lost respect for ancient law. You know that it has misunderstood love and has polluted marriage. You know that at great crises it demands a new law, a love more pure, bonds greater and stronger. Come to my aid, and impart to me your enlightenment, you whom a ray from heaven has transfigured. United in holy affection, let us proclaim, by our happiness and by our virtues, the will of God on earth. Be my companion, my sister and my wife, O inspired, dear daughter! Reveal to me the celestial thought you sing with your lyre. Leaning one upon the other, we will be strong enough to confound all errors and all the lies of false prophets. We will be the apostles of the truth. We will teach our corrupted and despairing brothers the joys of faithful love and the duties of the family.

HELEN, *playing the lyre*: Listen, O Spirit of the Lyre! Here is a sacred song, a beautiful and noble harmony. But I hardly comprehend it, for it is a voice from the earth, and for long my ears have been closed to harmonies of the earth. The silver strings no longer sound. The strings of steel have become mute. Explain to me the hymn of wisdom, you who have descended from the sky among men.

SPIRIT OF THE LYRE: I can explain nothing more to you, O daughter of the lyre. I can only sing of love. I have lost knowledge of science. I have lost it with joy, for love is greater than science, and your soul is the universe where I wish to live, the infinite into which I wish to immerse myself. Wisdom tells you of works and of duties, wisdom tells you of wisdom. You have no need of wisdom if you have love. O Helen, love is the supreme wisdom. Virtue is in love, and the most virtuous heart is that which loves most. Daughter of the lyre, listen only to me. I am a living melody, I am a devouring fire. Let us sing and burn together, let us be an altar where flame feeds flame; and without mingling with the impure flames that men set afire on the altar of false gods, let us nourish each other, and let us be slowly consumed until, exhausted by happiness, we mix our burned ashes in the rays of the sun that makes the roses flower and the doves sing.

ALBERTUS, *to Helen*: Alas. You answer me with a sublime song that lights in me a desire more and more vast. But sympathy does not put your song in rapport with my prayer. Leave the lyre, O Helen! You do not need melody. Your thought is a more harmonious song than all the strings of the lyre, and virtue is the purest harmony man can exhale toward God.

HELEN, *touching the lyre*: Answer me, O Spirit, O you whom I love and who speak the language of my spirit! Will our love be eternal and will death make no break at all in our marriage?

Not in the ray of the sun, nor in the flower of roses nor in the breast of doves can I extinguish the love that consumes me. I feel it rise toward the infinite with a consuming ardor. I can only love you in the infinite. Speak to me of the infinite and of eternity, if you do not want the last string of my soul to be broken.

CELESTIAL SPIRITS: Infinite Goodness, Eternal Love, protect the daughter of the lyre. Do not let the brilliance of this divine fire be extinguished in the sufferings of agony. Celestial Pity, shorten the trial of the Spirit, our brother, who languishes and sings on the brazen string. Open his breast to the children of the lyre, let a crown fall on the brow of the martyrs of love!

SPIRIT OF THE LYRE, *to Helen*: What does it matter for you to possess infinity? What need do you have to be assured of eternity, if, for a day, for an hour of your life, you have understood and have dreamed of both? Love alone can give this hour of ecstasy. Benefit from it, Helen, and let not ambition for an ideal future make you neglect the only instant when the ideal is present to you. Is not this instant enough and cannot love sum up in one minute all the joys of eternity? O Helen, to obtain this instant, I have watched with joy the breaking of all the strings that bound me to the sky by faith and hope. Only love has been left to me, and love is enough for me. Give me this instant, Helen, and if I am eternal, I consent to make sacrifice of my eternity. I consent to be extinguished in your soul, provided that your soul consents to receive mine and that it forgets, for a single instant, infinity and eternity.

ALBERTUS: You are silent to me, my poor Helen! The terrible sounds of the lyre draw you more and more toward the region of unknown thoughts where I cannot follow you. Take pity on me, take pity on yourself, O young prophetess! Fear this sacred delirium, too powerful for human nature. Come back to gentler thoughts, to a more humble faith, to a more deserving and kindly love.

CELESTIAL SPIRITS: O thrice holy! O a thousand times good and pitying one! Protect the daughter of the lyre, take pity on the Spirit of the Lyre.

HELEN, *playing the lyre with an impetuosity steadily increasing*: This is the result, I must love. Heaven and hell have illumined in me inextinguishable flames. My soul is a tripod filled with embers and perfumes. I would love you, O unfortunate sage, patient martyr of virtue and charity! I would love you, O Spirit of the Lyre, intoxicating melody, subtle flame, dream of harmony and beauty! But both of you speak to me of finite things, and the love of the infinite devours me! The one wishes that I love to serve as an example and instruction to the inhabitants of the earth; the other wishes that I love to satisfy the desires of my heart and to taste the goodness on the earth. O God! O Thou whose life has neither beginning nor end, Thou whose love has no limits, it is Thee alone I can love! Take my soul now or let it languish here in an agony as long as the existence of the earth. I will not destroy the love of the infinite. O my God, have pity, for I suffer. Love me, for I love you. Give me life, for I . . . (*The brazen string breaks with a terrible sound. Helen falls dead, and Albertus faints.*)

CELESTIAL SPIRITS: Glory to God in the highest heavens and peace on earth to men whose heart is pure! Spirit our brother, your trial is ended. Daughter of the lyre, your faith is rewarded. Come to us, children of love! Let a celestial marriage unite you for eternity! Glory to God in the highest!

SPIRIT OF THE LYRE: Where am I and what do I see? I awake in the heavens, and my vision embraces the infinite! Celestial light and imperishable love are granted me. O daughter of the lyre, your father has saved me. Come partake of infinite liberty and eternal joy! Glory to God in the highest! (*Helen is swept up toward the heavens with the Spirit of the Lyre and the Celestial Spirits.*)

ALBERTUS (*Raising himself up, he picks up the lyre and rushes wildly around the room.*): The lyre broken, Helen dead, dead! Helen! Helen! Where are you? I am your assassin! Helen, Helen! I want to kill myself. . . . Let me kill myself! . . .

MEPHISTOPHELES, *revealing himself before Albertus in his true form*: Do not kill yourself as you wish, my Master. You must truly expiate this little mistake. You will live, if you please, in my society, in company with despair.

ALBERTUS: Ah! Again this horrible apparition. Who are you, Spirit of Darkness, image of perversity, of atheism and grief? I cannot bear your looks. My God, deliver me from this vision. My spirit fails!

MEPHISTOPHELES, *approaching to seize him*: It will be necessary, however, for you to get used to it. The lyre is broken, and I have all power over you!

SPECTER OF HELEN, *appears to Albertus with the Spirit of the Lyre, under the form of two angels:*[48] Virtuous man, fear nothing of the tricks of the demon. We watch over you. Death destroys nothing; it binds up the bonds of immaterial life. We will al-

---

48. Goethe's *Faust*, part 1, ends with the death of Marguerite; Mephistopheles declares her doomed, but a voice from on high announces she is saved, and Faust is led off by Mephistopheles. Berlioz, in his operatic version (1854), adds a Chorus of Children, Gounod (1859) a Chorus of Angels. Sand's final scene rather resembles the end of some plays by Euripides, especially *Orestes*, in which Helen appears in the sky with Apollo and is to be taken off, at Zeus's order, for immortality with her brothers, Castor and Pollux, in the constellation Gemini.

ways be with you. Your thought can summon us at any hour. We will help you chase away the terrors of doubt and bear the trials of life. (*Albertus falls on his knees.*)

CHOIR OF CELESTIAL SPIRITS: Desist, Satan! You have no power over one who derives wisdom from faith and charity. His hand broke the six strings of the lyre, but his hand was pure, and the song of the seventh string has saved him. From now on, his soul will be a lyre whose strings will all resound to faith, and whose canticle will mount toward God on the wings of hope and joy. He has loved. Glory to God in the highest!

SPIRIT OF HELEN: And peace on earth to men of pure heart!

(*Mephistopheles flies off, grazing the earth, while the Celestial Spirits disappear into the skies.*)

Scene Four

Albertus, Wilhelm, Hanz, Carl.

HANZ: Master, Master, the hour for the lecture has sounded. They await you.

WILHELM, *nervously*: I expected to find Helen with you.

ALBERTUS: Helen has left.

HANZ: Left? Seized by a new attack of insanity?

WILHELM: What do I see? The lyre broken? Oh, my God! Where then is Helen?

ALBERTUS: Helen is cured!

CARL: By what miracle?

ALBERTUS: By the justice and goodness of God!

WILHELM: O Master, what do you mean? What has happened? We heard a terrible noise, like a clap of thunder. We see the lyre deprived of all its strings, and your face is streaming with tears.

ALBERTUS: My children, the storm has burst, but the weather is serene. My tears have flowed, but my brow is calm. The lyre is broken, but the harmony has passed into my soul. Let's go to work!

THE END

 *Select Bibliography*

EDITIONS

Sand, George. *Correspondance*, vols. 4, 5. Edited by Georges Lubin.
Paris: Garnier, 1968, 1969.

————. *Les sept cordes de la lyre*. *La Revue des deux mondes*, 15 April
(acts 1 and 2) and 1 May (acts 3–5) 1839.

————. *Les sept cordes de la lyre*. Paris: F. Bonnaire, 1840.

————. *Les sept cordes de la lyre*. Paris: Perrotin, 1842–44.

————. *Les sept cordes de la lyre*. Paris: Garnier, 1847.

————. *Les sept cordes de la lyre*. Paris: Hetzel-Lecou, 1852–55.

————. *Les sept cordes de la lyre*. Paris: M. Lévy, 1856–57; new ed.,
1869.

————. *Les sept cordes de la lyre*. Introduction by René Bourgeois.
Paris: Flammarion, 1973.

BIOGRAPHIES

Curtis, Cate. *George Sand: A Biography*. Boston: Houghton Mifflin,
1975.

Edwards, Samuel. *George Sand: A Biography of the First Modern, Liberated Woman*. New York: David McKay, 1972.

Jordan, Ruth. *George Sand: A Biography*. London: Constable, 1976.

Karénine, Wladimir. *George Sand, sa vie et ses oeuvres, 1804–1876*. 4
vols. Paris: Plon, 1899–1926.

Lubin, Georges. *Album Sand: Iconographie réunie et commentée*. Paris:
Hachette, 1952. Translated by Gerard Hopkins. New York:
Harper, 1953.

Maurois, André. *Lélia, ou la vie de George Sand*. Paris: Hachette,
1952. Translated by Gerard Hopkins. New York: Harper, 1953.

Sand, George. *My Life*. Translated and adapted by Dan Hofstadter.
New York: Harper and Row, 1979.

Schermerhorn, Elizabeth W. *The Seven Strings of the Lyre: The Romantic Life of George Sand*. Boston: Houghton Mifflin, 1927.

Winwar, Frances. *The Life of the Heart: George Sand and Her Times.* London: Hamish Hamilton, 1946.

OTHER STUDIES

Atwood, William G. *The Lioness and the Little One: The Liaison of George Sand and Frédéric Chopin.* New York: Columbia University Press, 1980.
Bakunin, Jack. *Pierre Leroux and the Birth of Democratic Socialism, 1797–1848.* New York: Revisionist Press, 1976.
Baldensperger, Fernand. *Bibliographie critique de Goethe en France.* Paris: Librairie Hachette, 1907.
_____. *Goethe en France.* Paris: Librairie Hachette, 1920.
Bourgeois, René. "Les deux cordes de la lyre, ou Goethe jugé par George Sand." In *Hommage á George Sand,* edited by Léon Cellier, pp. 92–100. Paris: Presses universitaires de France, 1969.
Butler, E. M. *The Fortunes of Faust.* Cambridge: Cambridge University Press, 1952.
Cellier, Léon. "Baudelaire et George Sand." *Revue d'histoire littéraire de France* 67 (1967): 239–59, esp. 246–47.
Evans, David Owen. *Social Romanticism in France, 1830–1848.* Oxford: Clarendon Press, 1951.
Greene, Titania. "Women and Madness in the Work of George Sand." *George Sand Papers* (Hofstra University Cultural and Intercultural Studies) 2 (1978): 59–69.
Marix-Spire, Thérèse. *Les romantiques et la musique: Le cas George Sand, 1804–1838.* Paris: Nouvelles éditions latines, 1954.
Newmann-Gordon, Pauline. *Hélène de Sparte, la fortune du mythe en France.* Paris: Debresse, 1968.
O'Brien, Dennis. "George Sand and Feminism." *George Sand Papers* (Hofstra University Cultural and Intercultural Studies) 1 (1976): 76–91.
Pailleron, Marie Louise. *François Buloz et ses amis: La Revue des deux mondes et la Comédie française.* Paris: Firmin-Didot, 1930.
Van Runset, Ute. "George Sand et Goethe: Histoire d'un malentendu." *Présence de George Sand* 23 (1985): 19–24.

Index